W9-CZM-252

COURAGE
TO BE
HEALED

COURAGE
TO BE
HEALED

MARK RUTLAND

CHARISMA
HOUSE

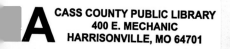

Most Charisma House Book Group products are available at special
quantity discounts for bulk purchase for sales promotions, premiums,
fund-raising, and educational needs. For details, call us at
(407) 333-0600 or visit our website at www.charismahouse.com.

COURAGE TO BE HEALED by Mark Rutland
Published by Charisma House
Charisma Media/Charisma House Book Group
600 Rinehart Road, Lake Mary, Florida 32746

Visit the author's website at drmarkrutland.com.

Library of Congress Cataloging-in-Publication Data:
An application to register this book for cataloging has been submitted
to the Library of Congress.
International Standard Book Number: 978-1-62999-647-9
E-book ISBN: 978-1-62999-648-6

19 20 21 22 23 — 9 8 7 6 5 4 3 2 1
Printed in the United States of America

To Dr. Dick Dobbins
Zikhrono livrakha
(May his memory be a blessing)

CONTENTS

FOREWORD

M Y FRIEND MARK Rutland has written a remarkable book that strikes right at the heart with the question "Do you have the courage to be healed?" Healing requires courage. It takes courage to recognize and acknowledge that we are hurt and need help. It takes courage to confront our pain and seek healing. It takes courage to forgive those who have offended and mistreated us. It takes courage to pursue peace and reconciliation. It takes courage to extend mercy and mend broken relationships.

When we consider the subject of healing, we must understand that this transcends physical healing. Often inner healing can be overlooked or bypassed with an overemphasis on the external; however, no amount of bandages can conceal what lies beneath. With this in mind, we must ask the question "Could there possibly be a deeper root, unknown to us, where we need healing and freedom?"

Today we have a larger number of people bound more

internally than externally. This is evident when you consider that suicide rates and prescriptions for antidepressant medications are at an unprecedented high. I write this with my heart breaking.

Healing is a choice—your choice.

Anyone who has used a trap to capture an animal knows an effective trap needs one or both of the following. First, it must be hidden in the hope that an animal will stumble upon it. Second, it must be baited to lure the animal into the trap's deadly jaws. Satan, the enemy of our souls, incorporates both of these strategies as he lays out his most deceptive and dangerous traps. These traps are both hidden and baited.

As I've traveled across the world, ministering in a variety of settings, I've observed one of the enemy's deadliest and most deceptive traps: offense. It imprisons countless Christians, severs relationships, and widens the existing breach between us. Often those who are offended do not even realize they are trapped.

Many are unable to function correctly in their calling because of the wounds and hurts inflicted by offenses. They are hindered from fulfilling their full potential and are producing the fruit of anger, hurt, outrage, jealousy, resentment, strife, bitterness, envy, and even hatred. Some of the destructive consequences of holding an offense are division, broken relationships, betrayal, and backsliding. People don't know they have fallen into Satan's trap.

Let's face it, Jesus made it very clear that it is impossible to live in this world without the opportunity to become offended. Yet even with this warning most believers are shocked and bewildered when it happens. They react out of an unrenewed mind instead of acting upon truth. This response leaves us vulnerable to a root of bitterness. Therefore, we must be prepared and armed for offenses, because our response determines our future.

Sadly we find example after example of offense, betrayal, and hatred among believers today. It is so rampant in our homes and churches that it is considered normal behavior. We are too numb to grieve when we see ministers taking each other to court. It no longer surprises us when Christian couples sue each other for divorce. Church splits are common and predictable. Ministry politics are played at an all-time high—often disguised as being in the best interest of the kingdom or the church.

Christians are protecting their rights, making sure they are not mistreated or taken advantage of by other Christians. Have we forgotten the words of Jesus?

> But I say to you, love your enemies, bless those who
> curse you, do good to those who hate you, and pray
> for those who spitefully use you and persecute you.
> —MATTHEW 5:44

This brings me back to the opening question: Do you have the courage to be healed? This is what separates those who find freedom from those who don't. Whether it's an offense or another issue, pride causes you to view yourself as a victim, keeping you from dealing with truth. It distorts your perspective and prevents you from having the change of heart—repentance—that will set you free. Although your true heart condition is hidden from you, it is not hidden from God. In addition to unforgiveness, root causes such as shame, fear, rejection, and condemnation must be exposed and eradicated.

True courage comes from vulnerability. Unless you're

willing to be honest about your current condition and courageous enough to lay hold of your healing, no amount of support, counseling, medication, or even prayer can adequately
help you. It is not enough to treat the symptom without
removing the root cause lurking within.

That's why I'm excited about this book. Mark doesn't just
dance around the surface—he dives in more in-depth and
cuts to the heart of the matter. Through *Courage to Be
Healed*, Mark imparts years of extensive research and leadership experience—along with the jolt needed for you to break
free, receive healing, and find freedom.

Let this truth sink deep in your heart: Jesus wants you
healed. Satan wants you to remain bound. Once you experience healing, your life will never be the same again!

Every epic story has a defining moment when the protago-
nist must summon the courage to overcome a challenge or
obstacle that will alter the course of his or her destiny.

This is your moment. How will it define you?

Embrace the courage to be healed!

—JOHN BEVERE
BEST-SELLING AUTHOR; MINISTER;
COFOUNDER, MESSENGER INTERNATIONAL

Introduction

YOUR COURAGEOUS MOMENT

WHETHER THE VIEW from a rooftop is beautiful or terrifying depends entirely on how safe you feel when you are up there. If you go up by way of the stairs on your own two feet, if you are sipping a cool drink and gazing thoughtfully over a lovely city scene, it feels one way—and that way is nice! If you are impaired and unable to walk, let alone climb the stairs, if while lying on your wretched prison of a bed, you are hauled up by friends and in constant danger of being dropped, the view will not be nearly so charming.

Now, suppose while lying there helpless, unable to rise and get down the stairs on your own, you watch in dismay as your friends violently rip a hole in the roof. Suppose it occurs to you that your friends have no intention of going back down those stairs at all. Instead, their plan seems to involve lowering you into the room below by ropes tied to the corners of your bed. It is a plan fraught with danger. What if they drop you? The thought of tumbling down the stairs was bad enough. The straight drop through the roof to the hard floor far below could easily mean the sudden end of your pathetic life. Living the rest of your days bedbound and paralyzed as you are is no happy thought. Death by sudden impact hardly seems an improvement.

With the roof now open, your friends tie ropes to the corners of your cot and turn their eyes to you. *"Ready?"* they seem to ask. It's a huge question, far huger than most allow. It's not just the danger. The room into which they are intending to lower you, safely or not, is filled with healthy people who do not understand your infirmity and will not be excited for your twisted self to become the center of attention. Neither, for that matter, are you.

You spend your life, such as it is, in the shadowlands of human existence. You are the crippled guy in the back room. You are the one someone else must care for and bring food to. You are the ghost in the family, the thing not well, not fully human, loved but mostly despaired of. You have been ignored or worked around all your life, and while hardly a warm or comforting existence, it is still better than being stared at with that familiar mixture of pity and horror. You have always feared exposure, been terrified when people look straight at you. You can almost hear what they are thinking: *"See him there. Look at how twisted he is, his limbs like knotted twigs jutting uselessly out from his miserably bowed spine."* Better to wait in the shadows for someone to remember you are there and bring you food.

And now these friends. They want to set you down right in the middle of the scene below. They mean well. They have faith. More than you do evidently. They have gone to no small effort to haul your useless body up here, and they are eager to lower you down. "Ready?" they ask. Yet they have no idea what they are asking of you. Are you prepared to be exposed, gawked at with barely smothered laughter and thinly disguised disgust? Are you prepared to be screamed at? Rejected?

"Get that thing out of here!"

They know and you know that Jesus of Nazareth is down there teaching. The room is packed with the well and whole, not with the likes of you. The thing is your friends and you have heard that this Jesus can heal the likes of you. Can He? Really? Will He?

The work and the faith to get you up here has all been theirs. The labor to lower you down without dropping you will be theirs as well. From then on, though, the risk is all yours. The hole in the roof awaits. The ropes are tied at the corners. Your friends are prepared to get you down where Jesus is. Now, this moment, this last, split-second decision whether to follow the plan to its end or retreat to the shadows, this moment is not about their faith. It is about you. The question of their faith and determination has already been settled. Faith was the challenge for them. They have answered well. Now, the question put to you is not about faith, not really. It is about something else entirely.

Your friends had the faith to get you up here even in the shape you are in. They have the ropes. Jesus is right there, right down in that room below. So close. Maybe your miracle awaits. Your friends believe it does. Now, the question for you is not about faith. Your question is different. *"Ready?"*

their eyes keep asking. Their question for you, their real question, whether they know it or not, isn't whether you have faith for a miracle. The answer to the faith question comes from one part of you. The real question, though, challenges a different part of you. The real question is this: Do you have the courage to be healed?

After fifty years of ministry and a lifetime of wrestling with myself, I have come to one great conclusion. The number one variable in the painful process of healing—and I'm speaking now of the healing of the soul, not the body—is not the skill of the counselor, though I humbly celebrate the abilities of the counselors I interviewed for this book. Theirs are special gifts of the Spirit, blended beautifully with techniques and methods acquired through decades of education and experience. They are used mightily of God to heal the wounded souls who, though not lowered through the rooftop, have arrived in their offices in need of healing.

Still, the skill of counselors is not the principal determining factor in inner healing. That factor lies within the wounded themselves. It is this: *courage.*

Think about it. The blind who came to Jesus for healing were courageous. They knew how to live blind. Living sighted, as good as it sounded, was unknown territory, and the unknown is always frightening. Because they had not seen for many years, the courage to see was not as small a thing as one might think. In the same way, a lame beggar has a certain way to earn his living, meager though it may be. His self-understanding is tied to his condition, as is the way others relate to him. All that is at risk if he gets healed. It may not seem like much, but risking all you have, all you know, and all you've ever known is a terrible, terrible risk.

Having the courage to be healed means facing reality as it is. How can I cry out, as did the wounded in the streets, "Jesus, Son of David, have mercy on me!" if I have never courageously faced my need for mercy? Settling for the appearance of wholeness is the easier path. The inner self, where the stuff of nightmares litters the filthy floor of the soul, is no country for cowards.

My own sojourn within myself, with all the detritus I have found there, has been harrowing enough to fill a book. Another book perhaps. Not this one. For this one I have gathered the experiences of Spirit-filled counselors who, after my promise to guard their identities, were willing to share their professional experiences. I then mixed in my notes from my own counseling of others. Rest assured, however, this is not the camp stew of chopped counseling with a few sexy root vegetables thrown in.

This is an anthem of courage. These are the stories of human pain met by God's healing grace. Each one of the individuals and stories here is absolutely real yet camouflaged beyond recognition. I have likewise blended and camouflaged the professionals whom I have interviewed. I made them into a solitary counselor with a single voice. The longer I worked on the material for this book, the clearer and more recognizable the voice and style of that counselor became to me. "Ah," I said, "so that is who he is. That is how he counsels the wounded, guiding them toward the truth that they have for so long and so desperately avoided."

Then I began to see the individuals. Each story, some so painful I could hardly bear to listen, became as real to me as if I had addressed it firsthand. In one case, as a university counselor shared a particularly tragic story, I began to weep. This unprofessional outburst took the woman aback.

"Are you all right?" she asked me.

"I just need counseling," I answered.

She stared at me for a moment and then said, "Oh, I see. That's humor, right?"

I said the people I interviewed for this research were brilliant. I never said anything about their sense of humor.

I record here in this book mostly stories of success, of those who were helped along by counselors, who were skillfully moved to higher ground. I could have saturated my readers with countless stories of failure, like the man who committed suicide just as he was making real progress. I could have told about the woman who drew a gun on her counselor and how the man was then forced to disarm her by breaking her arm. Or I could have described the young millennial woman who stormed out of a session after accusing her counselor of being an offensive quack—all because he dared to suggest her mother was a real person apart from being her mother and that her boss had the right to promote employees as he wished.

One counselor told me he felt 30 percent of his efforts were total failures, an absolute waste of time and money. Another 50 percent, he said, were marginally helpful in some limited and specific area. I remarked that left only 20 percent. "Ah, those," he said dreamily, "those make it all worthwhile."

A second counselor scoffed at 20 percent, declaring that no counselor with any integrity could claim such an inflated success rate. This rather curmudgeonly fellow claimed anything resembling success would be more like 5 percent.

This then is a book about them, that 5 to 20 percent who

bravely waded into the muck and mire, guided by counselors gifted and trained for the journey, and who came out on the other side freer and happier. I found that when I analyzed all the successes, all the stories and backgrounds and pain and progress, the various recipes for success had one ingredient in common. There was one factor that determined success or failure, one trait that lifted a troubled soul into the presence of a healing Savior and kept it there despite all pain and humiliation, despite all weariness and fear. That factor, that ingredient in the recipe of success, was the courage to be healed.

Chapter 1

THE POWER OF
EMOTIONAL POISONS

IN EUROPE IN the late 1800s two little boys were born at about the same time. They shared many things in common. Both had very strong, loving mothers. Yet these mothers were unable to overcome the domineering, violent, drunken ways of the fathers. As a result, both of these boys were often beaten and in ways almost too horrible to contemplate.

One little boy was pummeled so viciously by his father that he once spent three days in a coma hovering between life and death. It was a traumatizing experience. The other was routinely punched so savagely that he often had blood in his urine for weeks afterward. The mothers were not able to protect their sons—and deformities of soul set in.

Both little boys grew up to hold confused and distorted views of religion. They also experienced repeated failures early in their lives. One studied for the priesthood and never finished. He failed miserably. The other pursued the life of an artist and never neared acceptance. Both of these men lived their lives with a deep sense of shame. The rejection they had known from their fathers imprinted their souls with an enduring sense of unworthiness.

One of them was what might be called the "grandson of illegitimacy." Years before, a servant girl who worked in a Jewish household had become pregnant and then given birth. She never revealed who the father of the baby was. It may have been one of the other servants. Or it could have been one of the owners of the Jewish manor, a son or the father. This haunted the boy in our story. It tortured him that his grandfather may have been the illegitimate son of a Jewish landowner, which would have made this boy, in his own view, Jewish.

The child of a Jew who is the child of a Jew to the fourth generation would be Jewish. Living in the racist age that he did, this boy believed that if he was descended from Jews, he was in some sense dirty, flawed, and to be despised. This gave him a raging sense of self-loathing.

Both boys lived in confusion. Both were wildly disoriented in matters of religion. Both had a sense of being unloved and unlovely. Their deep poverty and their unending failures made them hate parts of themselves. They also felt that people who were like them, like what they feared themselves to be, had no right to live. This was the imprint of their fathers upon them.

There is a proverb—and it is correct as long as miraculous

healing does not intervene—that states, "As the twig is bent, so grows the tree." William Wordsworth, in his poem "My Heart Leaps Up," said it in another way: "The Child is father of the Man," or the grown woman.[1] In other words, in both negative and positive ways, we are the product of our childhood experiences.

These abused boys, then, determined to outstrip their shame. They determined to show that they were not what they feared themselves to be, what others had said about them all their lives. For example, one had a left arm that was stiff and unable to bend. He was also small for his age and unathletic. What did he do? He spent his life proving that he was not small and defenseless. He determined to be cruel, to become a mass destroyer.

The other spent his life proving that he was not the illegitimate child of a Jewish landlord. He devoted himself to proving that he was not defenseless, that he could kill rather than be killed, that he could maim rather than be maimed. He chose, then, to decimate millions, and he thus poured a philosophy of hate into the world that taints the souls of men to this day.

Perhaps you have already discerned whom I am talking about. That failed seminary student? His name was Joseph Stalin.[2] That beaten little boy who feared he was Jewish and failed at nearly everything he tried to do in his early years? His name was Adolf Hitler.[3]

Now, I can't leave these stories here. I have to reimagine their stories through the eye of faith and wonder what might have happened if these two boys had found the courage to be healed. How might history have been changed?

I know we have been raised to hate the names Stalin and

Hitler, and so it is hard to imagine any other scenario, any other results from their tortured lives. Yet what if someone had intervened? What if the love of God had brought these two tortured boys to a courageous moment when they welcomed the healing of their souls?

What if those little boys—violated, beaten, abused, rejected, unloved as they were—what if those little boys had found somebody to help them? What if when that boy studied for the priesthood there in his European country, one of those priests—instead of teaching him only the rules and the laws and the technical theology and the memory work—said to him, "God accepts you. God receives you. God loves you. God cares about you. Your heavenly father is different from the earthly father you have known"?

What if he had explained, "Your earthly father was in sin. Your earthly father was in bondage. He was probably a tortured, wounded little boy himself. He was probably a child in whom the twig was bent in a perverted way. But that cycle can stop in this generation because God loves you"? What might have become of that little boy? What might have become of that little boy in the other country if someone had said to him, "Look, why are you so obsessed with what you think is the nightmare of being the illegitimate child of a Jewish landlord? In Jesus Christ of Nazareth we all become the adopted illegitimate children of a Jewish carpenter"?

Maybe that boy born in Germany, who flunked out of art school and was terrified that he might be the illegitimate grandchild of a Jewish landlord, maybe he would not have spent his life killing six million Jews, all while trying to destroy that thing in himself that he hated.

Maybe if that other boy, the one named Joseph, could have

found the acceptance of God, he wouldn't have killed twenty million of his own countrymen and turned his nation into a police state, living his whole life in an attempt to prove that he wasn't the little crippled, rejected boy who hated himself.

What might have changed their story? What if someone had said to them, "Can you find the healing love of God? Are you able, somehow, to receive His acceptance at a high enough level to crowd out all the rejection you've experienced?" If only someone had taken Hitler and Stalin in his or her arms and said, "Look, you don't have to be the center of your universe. Christ can be the center of your universe and set you free from the driving demands of your tortured self."

In fact, let me share a thought I sometimes entertain. What if a young Hitler had stumbled into a Christian worship service when he was sixteen or seventeen? What if he had yielded his life to Christ? What if he had allowed the grace of Jesus to rescue his soul? What if all that energy and focus had been harnessed for the gospel? History might have been changed. It is hard to conceive, isn't it? Yet I wonder, if things had been different, if there might be a Christian college somewhere in Europe now with a plaque celebrating an alumnus named Adolf Hitler, the missionary who took Africa for Christ.

Strange to think this way, isn't it? And yet it might have been—if, that is, Adolf Hitler and Joseph Stalin had possessed the one thing essential to changing everything: the courage to be healed.

THE TOXINS OF OUR SOULS

As I said in my introduction, this book is an anthem to courage—the courage to be healed. I have been singing this anthem for years. I have sung it because I want to see believers set free. I have sung it because I believe we can reach a hurting world more effectively if we have first been healed of our own hurts. And yes, I have sung it because if God should allow us to intercept the lives of modern Joseph Stalins or Adolf Hitlers, I want to be part of that.

Of course, there has been opposition. Because I have long been an advocate for Christians to find the courage to be healed, to sit with skilled, anointed counselors and find wholeness, I have often heard the response I once received from a colleague. When I told him my views about counseling, he replied, "No one in the Bible ever went through counseling."

It struck me those years ago that not long after my conversation with this man he underwent gallbladder surgery. No one in the Bible ever had their gallbladder taken out either. It was all I could do to keep from reporting this fact to the fellow as he lay in recovery. The truth is that the "non-biblical" charge against counseling as an acceptable instrument of healing for believers is flawed, and it usually conceals some deep-seated fears.

It is time for us Christians to get real. We see the problems around us, problems of committed Christian people. It is time for us to ask ourselves some honest questions. Why does a born-again woman continue to battle depression? How can a Spirit-filled man act out sexually? That teenager who has repented and prayed to receive Christ as her Savior cannot continue to deeply, bitterly hate the uncle who molested her, can she? Can she still claim to be a Christian and medicate for shame and hate with alcohol? Of course not! We all know that. She has not really repented. She has not really gotten right with God. Everyone knows that. Don't they?

C. S. Lewis said that to understand sin and its destructive power, we need to look no further than the "zoo of lust" within us.[4] The same is true of the tangle of tortured emotions left behind by life's outrages. There is a zoo of deep emotional wounds within many of us that needs healing, and most of these wounds are concealed by long-standing deceptions.

Because I want this book to make a huge difference in your life, let me ask you this right up front: In what way have you been deceived? Were you, for example, molested as a child? Maybe the deception that haunts you is that you were partially to blame for that horrible moment in your life. In these pages I want to help you look at that deception, stare straight at it, and denounce it for the vile lie it is. This damage to the soul and concealing deceptions are what I call toxins. My goal here, and the goal of all good counseling, is to help you come to grips with the source of these toxins and then work out the healing that I know from long experience is possible.

Let me ask you to do something unpleasant. Let me ask you to consider the patterns in the brief descriptions that follow.

> Davie was rejected by his father. Later in life Davie gave himself to what some have called a "partying spirit." Buying acceptance through activities that he knew to be contrary to his deepest convictions, Davie compounded his rejection with guilt. He found a group of people who let him party with them. As long as he acted the way they wanted, valued what

they valued, he had buy-in with them. He was self-medicating his loneliness. Davie knew that if he revealed his true inner convictions to this crowd, all of his acceptance would be lost. And he would suffer even more rejection than he had already known in his life.

Bill also experienced deep rejection in his early years, and this left him with torturous insecurity. He medicated with work. Bill felt that if he worked harder, if he could strive more earnestly, then somehow or another he would earn enough acceptance to drown out the screaming inner voice of rejection.

Margaret lived her life behind a shell. Like a whipped dog, she felt ugly, unloved, rejected, and unworthy. Nobody could ever love her; therefore, she hid from the pain of this knowledge by living behind a shell of her own construction. She deliberately made herself less appealing, less winsome, less attractive, and ultimately less a part of society. In everything she did, she begged to be rejected. She deserved it. She knew that she was going to be rejected, so she established patterns of behavior that caused it. She acted in ways that were designed to make others reject her, that were useful to reinforce her own sense of her unworthiness.

Carlton was, in a word, overbearing. He was a conceited, arrogant know-it-all. By rejecting others, Carlton medicated his own sense of rejection. By making others feel stupid, he hoped to make himself feel smarter. By rejecting others, he hoped to make himself feel less rejected. His tactic was the preemptive strike. Of course, none of this worked for him. He simply made himself miserable by trying to make everybody else miserable. The truth is that Carlton was in agonizing and constant pain.

Robert's rejection led him into the egocentric life. He became rebellious and self-serving. He specialized in all the hyphenated sins. He was self-pitying and self-centered. He became the center of his own life. His nerves were on the outside of his body. Everything offended Robert. If it rained on his birthday, God was the author of some cosmic conspiracy to destroy his life. If Robert was in the living room and somebody slammed the screen door in the back of the house, Robert would jump to his feet and scream, "What do ya mean by that?" Everything was about Robert. He lived at the center of his own universe. At first it led to deep rebellion. Nobody had the right to tell Robert what to do. Nobody had the right because he was the center of his own world. This, of course, led to lying and ultimately to all kinds of deception, envy, and malicious gossip. Robert became unable to form mature relationships. He was unable to give or receive love. The egocentric personality cannot really love because love is about giving. He could not build lasting relationships. Hypersensitivity eventually frustrated his every effort. All friendships and three marriages were destroyed to prove the point.

Donny was a combative personality. He was always angry, always embroiled in a fight. Somebody was always "doing him wrong." His temper was just under the surface. Donny lived, as it says in Ephesians, with "bitterness, wrath, anger, [and] clamor" (4:31). At the same time, he was constantly excusing himself.

"I just have a temper."

"This is just who I am."

"Like it or leave it."

"You can't let people run over you."

Donny could not imagine that this pattern of anger and strife was observable by everyone else in his life. Donny could have an argument in ten rooms in a row, but when he came into the eleventh room, he started over fresh. He seemed to have no memory of the last ten fights. Somehow this all seemed normal to him. Now, everybody else saw this as a pattern, the witness of a bitter, combative personality. Donny was oblivious. He just thought that what he was experiencing was normal, life as he was made to live it.

Now, let me tell you something that will likely disturb you. All these people are real, and all of them are Christians. I could describe hundreds more like them. The core fact of their lives is one of the core facts I want to impress upon you repeatedly in these pages. You can be saved. You can be filled with the Spirit. You can love Jesus. You can read the Scriptures. You can experience God's grace in a thousand areas of your life. It is still possible, though, with all this being true, that you might have toxins in your soul, ruining your life.

Here is the all-important and yet often misunderstood truth: Salvation does what it does. It forgives us our sins and puts us in right relationship with an eternal God. It does not make us perfect. It does not heal all our hurts or all the unexplainable behaviors that are so contrary to what we believe.

It does not necessarily make us whole. In the same way, the infilling of the Holy Spirit empowers us for ministry and opens us to His sanctifying grace at a whole new level. It may not resolve our every inner conflict. It may not heal our every twisted memory.

The born-again, Spirit-filled believer may still need healing, the kind of healing needed for tangled emotions and hurting, damaged memories. This need for inner healing does not invalidate the glorious work of salvation. Instead, it is to say that God's desire for His children is wholeness, yet His healing grace works through His Word, in prayer, in counseling offices and at revivals, as well as in the instantaneous works of the Holy Spirit so many of us have experienced. We need not choose one means of grace to the exclusion of all others. God wants us whole.

Whole people are not just angry, hurting, depressed individuals whose sins are forgiven. Whole people are not people who sin and then tearfully repent in church and then sin some more. Our Catholic friends often mock the same pattern in their midst. A Roman Catholic may sin, then go to confession, then say a certain number of Hail Marys, and then go out and sin again. The next week the pattern is the same.

No, a whole person is not just forgiven for sins he or she uncontrollably keeps committing, like the people I just described. A whole person is changed. A whole person is fixed. A whole person has the damage removed. A whole person is free of the imprint of the horrors visited upon them. This is what God is able to do, but He often does it in places other than tearful worship services or dramatic public ministry. He is, after all, the Wonderful Counselor, and He often chooses to heal our lives through people who have been made wonderful counselors by His Spirit.

The good news here is that we can be free and whole, not just forgiven for patterns that never change. The challenging news for many of us is that God works this victory in our lives through processes that involve other people, some hard soul work, and, yes, the courage to be healed.

Max Cleland, a decorated war hero, US senator, and veterans' health advocate, made an interesting observation. He said that soldiers are trained to be strong, to fight on through painful wounds. This very strength may actually inhibit them from seeking counseling. The institution itself, the military, may need a new mindset with regard to the inner needs of its personnel.

As Senator Cleland told *Parade Magazine* in the October 4, 2009, issue in an article titled "Helping Soldiers Heal," "asking for help is counterintuitive for a soldier. I think it's imperative to change the military culture or at least understand that people can be broken. Just like vehicles, aircraft, or any other machine, soldiers have to appear for maintenance."[5] Senator Cleland might just as well have been speaking of the church. The body of Christ, especially that part of it in leadership, must come to experience a profound culture shift. Believers can be saved and broken at the same time. Ministers can be anointed and emotionally wounded at the same time. In fact like soldiers, Christians, particularly those in ministry, may "fight through the pain" until a meltdown eventually occurs. Then, of course, the damage may be even more devastating.

In my years as a minister and a university president, I've seen many believers suffer from inner conflicts that could not be reached and healed by repenting. It was hard to watch.

They would suffer from some inner deformity. They would repent, usually sincerely and tearfully. Little change would come. I also saw in myself deep unresolved pain that kept fighting its way to the surface no matter how well I preached or how successful my leadership was. I was saved, filled with the Spirit, and fighting a losing lifelong battle that cost me and those around me more than I could bear to watch.

I am now convinced that Christians, even ministers and priests, can, like soldiers, be broken. True believers, even people of great faith, can need to "appear for maintenance."

MURDERERS' ROW

The 1927 American League baseball season began at Yankee Stadium when the Yankees beat the Philadelphia Athletics.[6] It was the first win of an unforgettable season. The power of the Yankees' batting lineup was so intimidating to opposing pitchers that it was nicknamed Murderers' Row.[7] The 1927 Yankees scored 975 runs.[8] Batters such as Babe Ruth and Lou Gehrig hit sixty and forty-seven home runs, respectively.[9] The team batting average was .307, and its slugging average was .489.[10] In addition to the team's awesome power at the plate, the 1927 Yankees stole many bases. The Yankees' Murderers' Row lineup was one of the most celebrated in sports history.[11] There is another murderers' row. It is a lineup so intimidating, so utterly terrifying that it leaves emotional devastation in its wake. The core of this heartless lineup is so strong that its victims are battered into submission. Many a "pitcher" has gone to the mound with high hopes, only to be pounded into despair.

This is the "murderers' row" I want to expose and bring

healing from in this book. Those in this lineup are tough opponents and have left many who challenged them emotionally shattered and enduringly defeated. Yet they can be bested. Here they are:

- shame
- unforgiveness
- rejection
- condemnation
- fear

There is no question they have often beaten the best and brightest. Most "pitchers" of every age, station, gender, and nation have fallen to these "murderers."

There is only one pitcher who can strike them out: the Wonderful Counselor. Knuckleballs, fastballs, curves, and sliders are no good here. This is the realm of the mind, the stadium of damaged emotions in which the "murderers' row" is determined to steal, kill, and destroy.

We need a champion on the mound, a hurler who can strike out fear and defeat condemnation. We cannot beat rejection without a champion on the hill. The Bible puts it this way: "Who may ascend into the hill?" (Ps. 24:3).

That's a baseball question if there ever was one. Who's on the hill today? Call the bull pen. Who will ascend into the hill? Who will win for us this blessing, *all* the blessings of healing? Who can best the murderers' row that has tainted our triumphs, stolen our courage, and ravished our inner selves? It's a baseball question *and* a Bible question.

The Bible also answers: "He who has clean hands and a pure heart" (v. 4).

There can only be one. All others have at some time dirtied their hands and harbored impurities in their hearts. Only one is sufficient to the task. Only one meets this requirement. He walked alone out to the mound. The home crowd waits breathlessly. Can their champion prevail?

In the visitor's dugout the leering, mocking opponents wait their turn. They will do to this man on the mound what they have done to all men. He is no different. Then comes the announcement from the press box: "Now pitching for wounded, hurting humanity, the Wonderful Counselor. Tremble now, ye warriors of the night; the Son of Righteousness is risen with healing in His wings."

Let us now allow Him to do His mighty work in our lives.

A BLUEPRINT OF FREEDOM

Imagine a terrifying gorge, a deep and dismal canyon from which emanate gases lethal to the human soul. Through this noxious defile all humanity must pass. No one strolls unscathed in constant sunlight along the canyon rim. Deep in this ravine, hidden from the human eye, are five enemy dominions, principalities of death bent upon the destruction of the human soul. For each dominion there is a throne. These thrones, on the canyon floor, are the seats of deadly power from which the toxic vapors flow. Each of the five thrones emits a specific poison, and each poison derives its power from the throne.

All these five gaseous poisons that find access to a human soul draw it inexorably down toward the bottom of the gorge.

Once there the presiding throne locks the poison in. These toxins are deadening indeed to the human soul, but the throne of that toxin is the dead bolt. The hope of soul restoration lies not alone in treatment for the poison. That must come, of course. Antidotes must be found and absolutely must be administered. Vigilance must be maintained. These poisons are opportunistic enemies awaiting some sign of weakness as the signal to attack again. The greater hope, the greater grace for restoration, goes beyond the toxins themselves. It is the thrones that must be toppled. The soul's true hope of enduring restoration is the tearing down of the ring of thrones.

Following is a graphic that depicts all this. You will see on this graph that there are five toxins. Each one rests upon a throne, and for each throne there is a therapy, a healing grace. Shame, for example, which is not the least of the toxins, rests on the throne of deception. You will see in the pages ahead how the toxin of shame, resting as it does on a lie or on many lies, can only be dethroned by truth. In each case there is a toxin, a throne, a healing therapy, and always a goal. These form a blueprint for freedom. Look for this progression in each of the chapters that follow.

Each of the five toxins diagnosed and dealt with in this book rests on a throne, a dominion that gives it power to savage the sons and daughters of Eve. Underneath each throne there is a master lie specific to the throne, and each lie must be defeated by something greater—a biblical truth—for healing to happen. That's what true biblical counseling is really all about. Wounded souls in whom these toxins flow so bitterly must be detoxed by truth and truths specific to the toxin.

It looks like this:

TOXIN	THRONE	THERAPY	GOAL
Shame	Deception	Truth	Integration
Unforgiveness	Justice (judgment)	Grace	Mercy
Rejection	Doubt	Trust	Acceptance
Condemnation	Idolatry	Worship	Balance
Fear	Pain	Love	Hope

So then, what does the toxin-free, healed life look like?

- When shame's throne of deception gives way to truth, the result is integration. I can now put all the pieces of my life, even the traumatic ones, together. I am now together!

- Unforgiveness healed by grace makes my life merciful. I no longer live under the lash of judgment.

- Rejection, born of doubt and treated with the therapy of trust, brings acceptance.

- Condemnation treated with the therapy of worship brings life into balance. Unbalanced emotions are the ragged edge of idolatry, and worship restores balance.

- Finally, fear tied to the throne of pain is cast out by love. And love gives me hope.

There, then, is the picture of emotional wholeness: a balanced and integrated life of mercy, acceptance, and hope. That's the goal, what we are supposed to be shooting for. That's the very plan of God for your life. That beautiful picture is not some idealistic, unattainable dream. It's the desire of God for your life. He wants all the misery, all the venom, gone. He doesn't want the painful ruination of toxic emotions flowing across your life like poison. He doesn't want even one tiny trickle of shame or fear or rejection flowing in your life. Those things are the works of your soul's dark enemy. God has a different idea for you. It's called freedom, and those whom the Son sets free are free indeed.

Chapter 2

THE TOXIN OF SHAME

TOXIN	THRONE	THERAPY	GOAL
Shame	Deception	Truth	Integration

I**N THE SUMMER** before his fifteenth birthday, Johnny was raped. Not fondled inappropriately. Raped. He was seduced by an older woman and then immediately after raped by her brother. This young man was led like a sacrificial lamb to the horror of his humiliation and confusion.

He never reported it. Why not? Why not go to the police? Instead, he lived in terror that those who had degraded him would tell. They threatened to. They mocked him without mercy, telling him that if they spread the word about what had happened, all the men in town would want him.

When school started only weeks later, Johnny, who had never played organized sports, went out for football. His reckless abandon and fierceness on the field won him the praise of his coaches. Still, Johnny lived in fear of exposure. He couldn't face it fully, so he made it work for him. He discovered a surprising rage just below the surface. He let it loose. It became the manner of his life. He threw himself into fist-fights and combative arguments, vented the seething anger within him at every minor or even imagined insult. Johnny became a land mine primed and waiting for the next heavy tread to set him off.

Dating also started that year. It was a chance to show he was not what those people said. He was determined to prove them wrong. No, Johnny was a boy, all boy, and he was more than prepared to demonstrate it. He was handsome and daring, even a bit on the aggressive side, and girls found him attractive in an edgy, dangerous way. He soon gained a reputation for pushing the envelope on a date. He was as sexually charged as any adolescent male and far more committed to proving his masculinity.

He would not be humiliated or intimidated. No one, no matter how strong or even how well armed, would ever again dominate him. As his young body found its full masculine form, the small-for-his-age boy of the junior high years yielded to a sturdy young man staring defiantly back from the mirror. That masculine athlete would never let anyone humiliate him. Never again.

The image in the mirror became ever more real. The frightened boy of years before became less real. Indeed, the shame-drenched child gradually, then totally, faded from view. He seemed gone in a puff of smoke. It was as if he had never existed. The strong, well-muscled stud the world saw now had never been abused. He couldn't have been. Maybe some wimpy little cream puff might lie there weeping and terrified while a powerful and dangerous man raped him. Not this strong young man in the mirror. It had, quite simply, never happened.

The memory became a dream. The dream became smoke. The smoke blew away in the winds of many years, until the boy who was raped just went away. Some like to call this a suppressed memory. But *suppressed* implies force, a downward intentional pressure. One thinks of holding a lid on a boiling pot. Suppression.

Johnny's story was not like that at all. He applied no conscious effort to erase the memory. He just outgrew it. Left it behind. Until, finally, it was gone. In fact, he began to doubt that it had ever happened at all. No. It had *not* happened. He was quite sure of that now.

He reinvented himself. He actually remembered another life, a different life. He remembered it so clearly that it crowded out that vicious, nasty afternoon in an older couple's bed. It was gone.

Profound religious experiences also came with Johnny's new life. These were very real and may very well have kept Johnny from more empty, abusive years. Still, something wasn't quite right. He could not seem to drill down into his mysterious sense of unworthiness. He believed God for forgiveness. He really believed. Yet there was always that feeling, way back in the recesses of his soul, that he was dirty. Nothing could seem to reach it. He could not explain where it came from, this sense of filthiness.

It may seem amazing that he never connected the dots. He couldn't. How could he? That horrible, unforgettable "other thing" was actually forgotten. Gone. True, Johnny's Christian adulthood was punctuated by bouts of depression, cold fury, hot tempers, and on-again, off-again addictions. He became the successful CEO of a substantial corporation, but the battle raging within him never quit. Eventually, though, it erupted through the walls of his brilliant career.

After an explosive marital crisis, which threatened all he had built, now suicidal, depressed, and shattered, Johnny finally agreed to enter counseling. His fear of it was almost debilitating. The very thought of counseling struck terror into his heart. Why? He couldn't imagine. What could a powerful, successful, brilliant executive have to fear from counseling? He honestly had no idea. The fear was real and haunting nonetheless.

The first few sessions were horrible. Weeping, guilt-ridden, and profoundly shaken by the nightmare his marriage had become, Johnny allowed the counselor to drag him to ever deepening levels of honesty. At first they only dealt with what had caused the immediate crisis. Devastation was the best word to describe what had happened. Johnny's recklessness was the initial issue, but the counselor refused to stop there.

The counselor pressed on, probing further. Fear, unreasoning terror, gripped Johnny. He began to hate his counselor. Why? What was he afraid of? He honestly did not know. He wanted his marriage, though, more than anything in the world. He discovered that the wild, desperate ache not to lose his wife drove him to go on, to keep going back and back and back.

Finally came the right question asked the right way at the right time. The hidden horror erupted, blasted loose from its silent, long-forgotten tomb. Johnny was shattered by the experience. An awakened memory burst out of him and onto the counselor like lava. The never told erupted in a heartrending emotional torrent of words and tears and bitter, bitter hate.

Finally, decades after the crime against him had actually been erased from his conscious mind, Johnny unleashed a tirade of hidden hurt on the very counselor who finally excavated it. What was the worst of it? Humiliation. Utter confusion. Absolute horror. Who was he? What was he? How guilty was he? And of what?

The humiliation of it was inexpressible and utterly unbearable. It was all a horrible nightmare that had bred a life of nightmares. The boy had known too much, too early, the wrong way. As the twig is bent, so grows the tree. That's the proverb.

All his learning and earning and striving and driving, and his whole angry life of combat with the elements, were an effort to never endure that humiliation. No one would ever, ever again humiliate him.

All this had to be dragged up, dredged up, and somehow dealt with. For that kind of human hurt to ever find wholeness and healing, the Wonderful Counselor is the only answer.

"And His name will be called Wonderful, Counselor" (Isa. 9:6).

A BIBLICAL COUNTERPART

There is a story, not so unlike Johnny's, in the New Testament. We began this book with it, and retelling it here may help you see Johnny's story in a different way.

A certain man, so twisted that he lay completely useless on his pitiful bed, was afflicted day after day, year after year. His friends, four of them, were determined to get him into the presence of the Wonderful Counselor. They simply would not be stopped.

After hacking away the roof tiles above where the Counselor sat speaking, they lowered their afflicted friend by ropes into the room below. The outside condition of this broken man was apparent to all. Only the Wonderful Counselor, though, could see the inner wounds, wounds that cried for healing before he could ever be a whole person. What horror had left its mark within? What outrage had so marred that inner self that the outward life manifested such sad disease?

It was not as though the outward life was of no concern, of course. Far from it. Wholeness is wholeness. It is meant for both the body and the soul. But the fount of many curses bubbled within this man, poisoning him from the inside out.

The Counselor began there.

"Son, be of good cheer; your sins are forgiven you" (Matt. 9:2).

What guilt within him held his outward life in crippling bondage? We cannot know. In fact, it would offer no further insight were we to know every sordid detail. The Wonderful Counselor knew that for this life, for his physical self to be whole, the inner self had first to be freed of disease.

How like so many he was. Suspended, dangling between heaven and earth. Twisting in the wind. Supported by those who cared but still needing touch beyond their capacity. He lay there on his bed of pain, depending on his friends to haul him back up if this turned out to be just one more moment of false hope.

We tend here to make a false conclusion. We love to celebrate the laws of healing. We are certain we know what they are. Yet if this poor man was crippled by his guilty soul, then aren't all handicapped bodies the outward result of hidden guilt? There is no reason to think so.

The Wonderful Counselor sees each life individually, one at a time—heart by heart, mind by mind. Each unique and uniquely in need. The Counselor's gift was that marvelous ability to start fresh with every encounter. To each wounded life, His wonderful counsel came precisely to the point of need with surgical precision.

"Arise, take up your bed, and go to your house" (Luke 5:24).

The man left carrying his bed. What a miracle! And no longer carrying his guilt—a far greater miracle!

Myopic little saints and doubters alike have dismissed spiritual and emotional healing as somehow less miraculous than physical healing. But the tangled barbed wire of the soul is far more dangerous to touch and more complicated to heal than a diseased body and reachable only by wonderful counsel.

The crippled man rose and walked at the mere word of the Counselor. But first, *first*, mind you, he had to hear wonderful counsel set him free of the guilt and self-loathing that indentured him to his past. He walked. Wonderful. He walked free of his guilt. Wonderful counsel.

Johnny's Shame

Johnny was raped, and his internalized misery became the defining and very nearly terminal factor in his life. His pain, the repressed nightmare within his psyche, was real but hardly unique. You see, the deepest wound in Johnny's emotional bank was shame. Shame causes terrible damage. Shame, especially from violent sexual humiliation such as he experienced, leaves in its wake a deep-seated sense of unworthiness.

In fact, for Johnny the term *unworthiness* really would not fully express it. He felt unclean. The word he struggled to say to the counselor was *nasty*. Once he had constructed a survival mechanism strong enough to handle the rape, he still could not suppress the sense of nastiness he felt about himself.

Johnny's sense of shame manifested itself as a deep-seated self-loathing, so deep in fact that he could not even identify its source. He could not identify the source of this self-hatred because to do so would have required him to excavate his past. He hated what had happened to him, hated the people who had done it, and hated himself for being weak. The shame of it never left him. It came at him in waves of depression and loneliness. The loneliness occurred because by keeping a part of himself hidden away—even from himself—he could not relate his experience to anyone, including his wife. A partial man, partially hidden, relates partially, and Johnny was a partial man.

Johnny finally came to the place where he no longer knew what he was hiding or hiding from. There was a threshold, a black moment when he would instinctively pull back. No further. No closer. Stop right there. Not even his wife was allowed to go inside. Gradually this depression, loneliness, and fear of being truly known took control of his life, like a wall, like a garage door that would suddenly, without warning, lower itself, until Johnny found himself inside alone with the remnant of what he called himself.

Shame was the root of his brokenness. In some ways he was a compassionate person. He cared for the poor, gave to worthy causes, and was known to be a kind and considerate boss. But he was not kind to himself. Johnny drove himself without limits. He never saw a doctor, never took care of his own health, and always took dangerous physical risks. His inner sense of unworthiness crowded out self-love and therefore self-care.

He was a partial man. Terrible secrets hid within and drove him to live and work at breakneck speed. Something seemed to pursue him day and night. In his nightmares, truly horrible nightmares, some powerful force always attacked him, chased him to the end of his endurance until he would awaken to his own screams. Awake or asleep, he could not escape it, but he had no conscious idea what *it* was.

Now we know. Now Johnny knows. It was our first toxin: shame.

Shame is perhaps the most destructive of all negative emotional forces. The kind of deep-tissue humiliation inflicted by sexual violence, for example, leaves a nearly indelible stain on the inner child. A sense of dirtiness lies on the life like a shadow. Indeed, shame is so terrible to bear that the shamed inner child informs the direction of the adult in virtually every aspect of life.

There are two principal reactions in lives wounded by shame. The first is a defeatist attitude. Those who respond in this way just never seem to be able to succeed at much of anything. Shame erodes their energy, devours their vision, and almost mysteriously limits all upward thrust in their lives. The emotionally wounded whose lives are suppressed by shame gradually come to sense that all their possibilities are under some kind of invisible ceiling.

They uniformly express a vague feeling that a smothering form, some oppressive blanket, blocks their every effort. They live out an acquiescence to marginalization in their fate.

What good is it to try very hard? They live half lives. They experience only partial success and shrug off one setback after another as simply symptoms of the force that controls their lives!

The other response to the inner wound of shame is combativeness. They become battlers like Johnny. Feeling the opposite of those who feel doomed to defeat, the battlers are drawn to a fight like moths to a flame. The beaten are smothered by shame; the battlers spend their lives hammering at it as at a stone wall. They can't earn enough or learn enough to bury their shame. No matter how far down they push, no matter how deeply they dig its grave, somehow shame works its way back to the surface. That is precisely why so many battlers have late career crack-ups. They fight and scrape with their own shame and virtually everyone and everything else until at some point the whole house of cards comes down, often at a moment of unsustainable success. The battle is too long, the resources too little. They do not so much lose as they outrun their supply lines.

It is important for us to know that each of the five dominions of emotional damage is seated in a "host throne." There is also a therapy for each one, capable of unseating it. Shame is seated in lies. The power that unseats shame is therefore truth.

V THE THRONE OF DECEPTION

Emotions tortured by shame are held in that bondage by lies. As long as the lies are believed, at a deep, even subconscious level, the hold of shame is tightened and strengthened.

There are vast armies of these lies that bind shame to the

soul both consciously and subconsciously. Here are the top ten I have observed. I call them "the ten lies that host shame's power":

1. This thing that happened left a permanent stain. Nothing can wash it away.

2. It must be kept from others, and it must be hidden.

3. You are what others did to you. You are what happened.

4. You can hide your shame behind a veil of success.

5. You cannot hide your shame no matter what you do. Everyone can see the stain.

6. You are partially to blame for this shame.

7. No one could ever really love or admire you if the person knew your shame. The only way to earn the admiration you long for is by weaving a veil of success to hide the shame.

8. You must be strong. Your personal strength can keep the shame under control. Only weaklings and failures let the shame they feel hamper their efforts.

9. There is little use in trying because you are never going to be much of anything.

10. There is something deeply wrong with you. There is something dirty about everything you are.

The Therapy of Truth

Thankfully there are answers for these lies. The medicine that must be swallowed in the healing process is truth. All Johnny's blindness to his pain, that cloud of denial under which he had lived for decades, had to be pierced, and it had to be pierced by truth. This process was his worst nightmare, and it was agonizing to watch.

He endured session after session, question after question, probing, always probing, further in. The closer Johnny got to the core, the angrier and more resistant he became. He lashed out at the questions, accused his counselor of being "no good at his job," and even felt waves of violent anger. What did this man want? What was he after?

Johnny could see something up ahead. He did not want to go there. Whatever it was, he did not want to see it up close. "Leave it there. Do not go up there," a voice screamed inside of him. "Stay back! Do not let this counselor take you there."

The counselor refused to quit. Questions. No accusations. No condemnation. Just questions. Calm. Firm. Unstoppable questions. Always with the questions.

At last they were at the dreadful place. There was one final door. Johnny's skin crawled. He begged, wept, refused at first, then finally submitted. The determined counselor simply would not stop. Quietly insistent, he helped Johnny push open that final, horrible door and step over the threshold back into the long-denied nightmare.

It was explosive. It was horrible to watch. Pathetic. A middle-aged man ripped the scab off of his most painful wound, and rage poured out like blood. The counselor just watched. He had never seen anything like it, not in all his years of treating the wounded. Finally, exhausted, Johnny wept pitiably. The rage now spent for the moment, hot tears poured down like acid rain.

What did the counselor do? What could he do? Wait and pray and comfort Johnny in that moment, knowing all the while some of the worst of the journey still lay ahead. The horrific details of Johnny's story poured out in alternating waves of rage and broken, sobbing humiliation.

It all poured forth except for one word, one terrible, unacknowledged word. Johnny could describe the event, at least he thought he could, but he steadfastly refused to name it, to call it what it was. The counselor tried to coax the word out of Johnny. Johnny declined, then refused to use it. Anger flared again and again when the counselor used that terrible, ghastly word.

Why?

Women are raped, not men, not in Johnny's mind. A lifetime of proving he was not a defenseless victim of rape threatened to come unraveled in a single word. If it was rape, who was Johnny? What was Johnny? All the sports, all the combative struggles, and all the testosterone-drenched conflicts of a lifetime began to look like the wasted outer battle of an inner victim in denial.

We should listen in now as the counselor takes Johnny ever closer to the truth that can set him free.

Counselor: If you do not want to call it rape, then what do you want to call it? Were you a willing participant? Did you want it? What should we call it if not rape?

Johnny: I don't know. No, of course not. No.

Anger rising. Close to exploding. *What does this counselor want me to say? Why? Why is it so important? Why do I have to say it?*

Now sobbing. Broken.

Johnny: He raped me. Together they humiliated me, and then he violently raped me. Is that what you want me to say?

Counselor: Is that what happened?

Johnny: Yes. Do we have to keep using the word?

Counselor: You will come to the place where you can use it without this level of pain.

Johnny: And shame. The shame is worse than the pain.

Counselor: Aren't they the same thing?

Johnny: You tell me. You're supposed to be the expert.

Counselor: The time will come when you will be able to use the word without shame. You will be able to look back on that day and see it for what it was. You were not guilty. You did nothing. What was done to you was someone else's sin. It was violent. Forced. You were a boy. Hardly more than a child. Think back. Small for your age, weren't you? He was a grown man. He threatened you. Call it what it was.

Johnny: Why?

Counselor: Healing for truth. Wholeness for honesty. Call it what it was, and you finally put the guilt where it belongs.

Johnny: I know what it was.

Counselor: Of course you do. Someday you'll be able to say it without feeling the shame.

Johnny: Maybe.

Counselor: Trust me. You will.

The wounded must come to see the truth and speak the truth. Having the truth spoken to them, at them, is not the same. They must be brought around to the therapy of speaking the truth. It truly does make free those who know it. Just not at first. Truth, at first, is the wound that heals.

The problem is that to the hurting such bitter truth can seem a cure worse than a curse. They cling to whatever little shred of shade they can find to hide from the truth's blazing heat. The wounded adore their comforting illusions and cling to them with stark, desperate tenacity.

Johnny did. Even after the cataclysm of opening up the locked closet, he continued to use such phrases as "since that day" or "when that happened" or "after what those people did." He later told the counselor that even in private, even in his own thoughts, he could hardly bear to call it more. The therapy of truth was loathsome medicine indeed for Johnny. But medicinal it was nonetheless.

Gradually Johnny began to take hold of the fact that the undercurrent of shame that had gripped at him for forty years was not his to endure. Why should he feel shame for someone else's shameful deed? If someone is robbed, is that person shamed, or is the robber? A beating victim is not shamed; the assailant is. A rape is a shameful thing, an act of violence, a deed of perverse shameful horror. But the shame, *all* the shame, is on the rapist.

THE GOAL OF INTEGRATION

Once the truth has been acknowledged, the integration of the self has to begin. This is essential. Johnny had sealed off a painful part of his life. It was the elephant that was in another room. That compartment was off-limits to his own psyche. He never went there. Not with his memory. Not in his conscious mind. Not even in prayer. He did not even "allow" God in that room. This mental task of compartmentalization "worked" for Johnny for a long time. By shutting the door on that dark, ugly room, Johnny mastered the art of compartmentalizing.

This coping mechanism builds walls between various areas of our conscious and subconscious mind, fracturing our lives in the process. A painful memory gets locked in a closet, and the fact that it is locked away actually feels good. We try it again—an inconsistent behavior here, anger and hurt there, until our mind becomes a maze of walls. Parts of our inner, emotional self stop connecting to other parts. The problem is predictable, of course, that the inner war to keep all the compartments locked in separate rooms will become a horrible strain. Some of the contents of these compartments are profoundly inconsistent with one another. The human mind can only maintain the distinction for so long.

Which compartment am I in now? Which compartments are the contents trying to get out of? I have been living in one compartment. Now I am in another, and the things I did or felt or experienced in the one compartment cannot be known in this new one. They cannot know about each other. I get confused. Depressed. The strain to keep the compartments separate becomes unbearable. I cannot keep it all sorted out.

Let's listen in again as the counselor helps Johnny with this very thing.

Counselor: Johnny, tell me about your level of anger.

Johnny: It's been a lifetime issue. When I was younger, it became explosive. My wife really suffered. Then the anger went away, and dark depression came in its place.

Counselor: The anger didn't go away.

Johnny: No?

Counselor: No. It just turned inward. Anger at yourself frequently manifests as depression.

Johnny: I've had plenty of both. Depression and anger.

Counselor: But you've gotten pretty good at not showing it in public.

Johnny: Very good, I'd say. I managed a pretty big company; I was popular with my employees. And after a bad bout with depression in my midthirties I had a great experience with God. I really felt all that was gone forever. It seemed to be. For years. Then lately the anger came again, but deep inside. Not hot anger but cold anger. I never yelled or threw things. I just withdrew.

Counselor: From your wife?

Johnny: Mostly. Any conflict. Any criticism. Sometimes over nothing. I would just go back inside myself, like a turtle. No, it was more like a shield coming down, all around me. At first I tried to fight it. It totally separated me. It was horrible. Like being in a tiny cramped phone booth or a glass cocoon. I could see out, but I couldn't reach out. Jenny would try to reach in, but all she got was that shield.

Counselor: Or a wall?

Johnny: OK, a wall.

Counselor: You see you were starting to build lots of walls. You walled off your private thoughts from your business. You walled off your inner self from your wife. You walled off your spirit from God. You walled off God and everyone else from your past. You even walled off your past from yourself.

Johnny: Yes, even myself.

Counselor: And God.

Johnny: And God.

Counselor: The unintegrated living is very broken.

Johnny: And depressing.

Counselor: Of course, Johnny. That's why you kept pouring things that felt good into the wound—business success, accomplishments, more and more and more. Nothing helped for long. Then you tried the destructive things, and that is when the anger and depression really multiplied. Add guilt to anger and depression, and you have a pretty potent poison. So you work even harder and build more walls until depressed, guilty, confused, and compartmentalized, you melt down. Your failures were a private compartment nobody saw. Nobody saw but Jenny, and you wouldn't let her in to help.

Johnny: No, I wouldn't.

Counselor: How do you think that made her feel?

Johnny: Rejected.

Counselor: Of course. Rejected in childhood and now rejected in her own marriage. That's pretty wounding.

Johnny: I guess I wasn't much of a Christian.

Counselor: You were a Christian. If you weren't, you would not feel the guilt and remorse you do. You were a Christian. You were deeply hurting inside, unintegrated, and self-medicating. You used "medication" that made every-thing worse, until finally you were cut off from the only two sources of real strength in a married man's inner life: his wife and his God. You stretched the surface of your life further and further, thinner and thinner, but you failed bitterly to fill the inside with anything of value. You became an empty shell. The crack was inevitable.

Johnny: Oh God, what have I done? I've wasted everything. *Weeping, sobbing.*

Counselor: Go on. Let it go. Those are cleansing tears, remorseful tears. It's no shame to cry for remorse, but at the end of the tears remember that you have not wasted every-thing. Not everything. Romans 8:28 is important here. That is your assignment. Memorize it.

Johnny: I know Romans 8:28.

Counselor: Well, memorize it again. Before we meet next time, I want you to meditate on what that verse means to you in this crisis season of your life. Think about what that scripture means in all this.

PATH TO WHOLENESS

Compartmentalized people gradually lose their sense of the totality of life. Things start to lose their meaning. Life becomes broken pieces. But then comes the good news: "All things…" Romans 8:28 speaks of a connected view of life in which all things touch. All things knit together in a single tapestry. There is a woven picture of the good and the painful and the impossible to bear. It is the opposite of what shame produces—life in pieces, lived in pieces by people broken into pieces, is nothing but pottery shards.

Wholeness is life without walls. It is "all things" worked together for good to them that love God and are the called according to His purpose (Rom. 8:28). Then, somehow, "all things" have meaning. My whole life, my great pain, and even death somehow "work together" for good.

Those who decorate houses use this phrase all the time. So do fashionistas. This one piece, this particular chair or sofa or scarf, may not be all that great, but the room "works together." For those who love God and are living a called purpose, the promise is that life does work together for good. God makes it work together. He takes all we surrender to Him, and He makes it work together for good. The caveat is obvious. He does this with "all we yield to Him." Whatever we wall off, whatever we keep back, will become abscessed. Separated, unconnected, and unsurrendered, it stands apart from the process of "working together for good." We have to put it in His hands.

The challenge is that we are reluctant to surrender what in our own eyes is "bad." I cannot really give God the terrible things done to me because they are too terrible even for God. I cannot let Him see it. Or more destructive still, I cannot surrender the evil done to me because God might take away my pain, and pain is what has defined me for so long that I cannot dare imagine life without it.

Furthermore, I cannot surrender the terrible things I have done because I cannot see how they could ever work together for good. My strength. My talents. Perhaps my pain. But never my sins. Those I must hold. Under that weight I must carry on. But let God weave them into a fabric that is beautiful? Never.

Johnny had to surrender both to move forward in his healing. He was deeply conflicted internally. His sins disgusted him, and his guilt was crushing. Even more than this, his adolescent outrage could not fit in to his life. He was a respected businessman, a successful person not easily taken advantage of. So in his mind he walled off that inconsistent moment of horror. It did not fit in his life as he had worked to create it and as he imagined it.

Johnny's acceptance of forgiveness for his sins and his ultimate ability to forgive what had happened to him wove the two together. Yes, he had been sinned against. Unspeakably. Yes, he had sinned in other areas of his life. At an emotional level the two were profoundly connected. It is too tight a linkage to call it a precise cause-and-effect relationship, but the connection between the two is undeniable. Therefore, connecting the two with forgiveness as well made a tapestry of destruction into a holistic pattern of healing.

The more difficult leap for Johnny was not forgiveness per se but embracing the moment of his outrage and his own failures as part of the picture. If "all things" really means "all things," then somehow what happened to him had to fit in the picture. So also did his own failings.

Let's tune in again as the counselor does his work.

Counselor: How about it? Did you work on Romans 8:28?

Johnny: Yes. But as I told you, I know it well.

Counselor: Quote it for me.

Johnny: What?

Counselor: Humor me.

Johnny: All things work together for good to them…

Counselor: That's it.

Johnny: Yes, that's it.

Counselor: Yes, that's it.

Johnny: I just said that.

Counselor: And you're correct. You have quoted it correctly, but you are not hearing me. That's it. That's where we have to go now.

Johnny: Where?

Counselor: To "all things." All things work together. All things.

Johnny: OK. All things. I'm not seeing this so far.

Counselor: Well, let's start with the end and work forward. Are you called to a purpose?

Johnny: Yes. Maybe. Once I was.

Counselor: Which one is it? Is there a calling on your life or not?

Johnny: I know there was. I pray there still is.

Counselor: There is. You still have work in the kingdom. Deep down, very deep in your heart, do you believe that?

Johnny: Yes. Honestly, I do.

Counselor: Good. Now the second part. Still working backward from the end of the verse, "them that love God." Do you love God?

Johnny: That I can answer easier. Yes, I have never loved God as much as I do now. I love God and my wife more than I ever have. I tried to serve Him. But I never loved Him as I do now. The same with Jenny. It's as though I have fallen in love with both of them, my God and my wife. I feel desperate to love them, truly desperate.

Counselor: Do you know why that is?

Johnny: I have no idea.

Counselor: Because you could not really love them before. Hidden people are not really free to love. Whole persons love wholly. You had parts of yourself locked away. Certainly God knew everything, but now it's out there, really out. As for Jenny, she didn't know. How can you love her with your whole heart when you cannot let her into your whole life? You didn't know before if she could love that hidden part of you. Now you know. And so does she.

Johnny: She has forgiven me for what I did, and she loves me for who I am.

Counselor: What a woman.

Johnny: Yes, what a woman.

"ALL THINGS" JOHNNY

Clearly, Johnny was finally able, with the help of his counselor, to pry open the locked door and enter in upon that long-suppressed scene of horror. Then he had to deal with how that scene fit in to his life. He had to see that the lack of a fit explained his periodic bouts with depression. He also had to see how it explained his many unexplainable failures. The adult Johnny began to get in touch with the wounded child of Johnny within.

Again, let's follow this progression with the counselor.

Counselor: Close your eyes and visualize that boy in the hour afterward.

Johnny: You mean myself?

Counselor: Yes, but don't think of him that way now. He is a boy. I want you to close your eyes and see him in that hour or so after this terrible thing happened. Can you see him?

Johnny: Yes.

Counselor: Describe him to me. Where is he?

Johnny: He is alone.

Counselor: Where?

Johnny: At a school playground near his house. It is Saturday, and everyone is gone. He is crying.

Counselor: Crying?

Johnny: Sobbing. His whole body is shaking.

Counselor: What is he feeling?

Johnny: Shame. He is ashamed. And afraid.

Counselor: Afraid it will happen again?

Johnny: No. He is afraid his friends will find out.

Counselor: He needs to be comforted, doesn't he?

Johnny: There is no comfort. He is alone.

Counselor: Why don't you comfort him?

Johnny: What are you talking about?

Counselor: Put your arm around him. Right now. Close your eyes and see that boy. Look at him there alone, hiding at an abandoned playground. He's afraid, isn't he?

Johnny: God, I don't want to see this anymore.

Counselor: Keep your eyes closed, Johnny. Don't stop. Look at him. Is he crying?

Johnny: Yes. I hate this. I can't stand this anymore.

Counselor: Hang in there, Johnny. You can do this. Embrace him. Take that little guy in your arms and comfort him.

Johnny: I don't understand.

Counselor: Sure you do. Keep your eyes closed and speak to him.

Johnny: And say what?

Counselor: What he needs to hear. You should know.

Johnny hesitates. He is now weeping himself. The counselor waits. At last Johnny speaks, barely above a whisper, as if he were that little boy, that boy who is actually himself.

Johnny: You're a boy. You're just a boy. What they did is not your fault.

Counselor: Go on, Johnny. Tell him more.

Johnny: This is stupid.

Counselor: No, it's not. Close your eyes and comfort him.

He hesitates again. The counselor waits.

Johnny: This doesn't mean anything about you.

Counselor: That's good, Johnny. That's real good. Go on.

Another wait, longer this time.

Johnny: There are bad people. Evil people. What they did to you was horrible, but it doesn't make you...

Counselor: What, Johnny? Doesn't make you what?

Johnny: Nasty.

Now truly weeping.

Johnny: This doesn't make you nasty.

Counselor: Good, Johnny. You take him in your arms. Embrace him.

Johnny: I don't...

Counselor: Sure you do. Gather him in and tell him, "I embrace you. I receive you."

Now sobbing.

Johnny: I embrace you. I receive you.

Counselor: That's good, Johnny. Keep on saying it for a while.

He repeats it several times.

Counselor: Now for the really important part, Johnny. Tell him this: "You are me."

He draws a deep breath.

Johnny: Yes, you are me. I embrace you.

Counselor: That's right, isn't it? Johnny, look at me. You see, he is you, and when you embrace and comfort the child within yourself, you start to find healing at a whole new level. The wall between your past and present is down. The boy within you is you. Today you embraced the child within.

Johnny: I'm exhausted. I want to quit.

Counselor: Of course you are. I'm so proud of you. We'll stop for today, but we won't quit.

HEALING SHAME

The thing about trauma is that it is traumatizing. I do not say this to sound frivolous. The truth is that a traumatic event such as what Johnny endured, as terrible and painful as it was, is nevertheless an event. It's of limited time. When it's over, it's over.

Only it isn't. The traumatic event may be over, but the traumatized life remains. Hurt, confused, frightened, and disoriented souls who have been through trauma, especially sexual trauma, need healing that goes way beyond, far deeper than, the physical. No medicine reaches the deep crevices of the soul. Such wounded souls need wonderful counsel. They do not need it just to get through the event. That is over. They need help to deal with the long-term damage done, and that damage most often manifests itself as shame.

Sexual trauma is a common source of shame, but it is far from the only source. For example, deep-tissue shame can also be the result of sin. The person, especially an otherwise respected person—a Christian leader perhaps—who commits what he or she sees as a particularly shocking sin can easily fall into shame. Shame can also be poured into the soul by the sins of others. A child can receive shame mouth to soul by parents who express disgust with something the child does or, far worse, something the child is. I am not speaking here of disapproval or correction. Shame oozes out of words such as "nasty" and "disgusting." Shame is the bitter harvest of seed phrases such as "You make me sick" or "You sick little creep."

The boy caught masturbating by his legalistic and hysterical mother may be scalded with a shame far darker and more destructive than the result of all his adolescent sexual fantasies. Shame drips from many a family faucet: the preacher's daughter pregnant out of wedlock, the prominent leader caught up in a scandal, or the teenager terrified his girlfriend will find out his mother is in the mental hospital. Shame is not embarrassment. Embarrassment is when you spill your spaghetti in your lap. Shame is soul poison, the devastating humiliation of disgrace.

There is another matter that needs to be said at this point, and it needs to be said firmly. Shame is a terrible wound that will be healed only with wonderful counsel. However, making someone ashamed is also a terrible, terrible sin. The religious appetite for public humiliation is demonic. The adulterous woman hurled at Jesus' feet was not nearly as wicked as her accusers. They cared nothing for her poor soul. To them she was barely human. She was just a thing—a wretched, sinful thing whom they hoped to use to destroy Jesus. Her redemption meant nothing to them. Her healing meant nothing. It never occurred to them. They believed she deserved her fate.

Let her sit there in the dust of her disgrace. She earned her shame. Let her wallow in it.

It was Jesus who showed her mercy. It was Jesus who healed her disease, took away her shame, and summoned her into a new and holier life. The religious leaders relished her shame. Jesus despised it. They magnified her shame. Jesus healed it. Shame that wounds His children hurts the heart of God. The self-righteous enjoy the shame of the fallen, but always remember this: it is demonic to enjoy what hurts the heart of God.

The Book of Genesis says that Adam and Eve were naked and were not ashamed. It does not mean "embarrassed," as some translations have it. It means shame. Shame had no place in Eden and no grip on the two healthy souls who dwelled there. It was deception that gave shame its first access and then gave it a stronghold in fallen humanity's wounded soul. Shame breaks mankind into pieces, robbing humanity of wholeness.

What then can unloose the horrible bonds of shame? What can tear down its throne and topple its dominion? Truth, of course. Not just true stuff. Not just facts or accurate data. *The* truth. "You shall know the truth, and the truth shall make you free" and whole and without shame—just as we once were in the garden (John 8:32).

The throne of shame is deception, and the lie underneath that throne is this: I am what someone has, or even I myself have, done. That is the source of shame, and shame is the bitterest toxin of all. Because it is the bitterest, its healing requires the greatest therapeutic truth of all. And that truth is "I am who He says I am."

Biblical counseling for shame rests on many great scriptures, but surely the greatest of these is John 1:12: "But as many as received Him, to them He gave the right to become children of God." Here is the truth that heals emotions damaged by shame, especially trauma: I am not what someone did to me. I am not even what I have done. I am who *He* says I am.

Chapter 3

---·◦✦◦·---

THE TOXIN
OF UNFORGIVENESS

TOXIN	THRONE	THERAPY	GOAL
Unforgiveness	Justice (judgment)	Grace	Mercy

I WANT TO TELL you some stories about people who were challenged to forgive wrongs done to them in their lives. I also want to ask you to ponder whether you face the same types of challenges to forgive, even if the circumstances are not the same.

Devon was a rancher. His father had carved the family ranch out of the prairie with his own two hands and then had proudly handed it on to his son. Devon gratefully tended it. The day he married and brought his new wife home to share his life on the ranch was one of the most glorious days he had ever known.

Then came the divorce. Then came the judge's order that the ranch be sold and the money divided between Devon and his now ex-wife. It got worse. The ex-wife bought out Devon's half of the ranch. The judge had ordered it. Now she was shacking up on the ranch Devon's father had built, and she was doing so with the very lawyer who had "gutted" Devon in the divorce proceedings.

Devon hated his ex-wife. He hated her lawyer lover. In fact, he hated the judge, he hated the ramshackle town house he had to live in now, and he hated the grimy little town it sat in, the one not far from the ranch he used to own. The ranch his father built and gave him. The ranch that should still be his.

How Devon hated.

Then there is Edith. Prepare yourself for this story.

Edith began seeing a counselor because she suffered debilitating depression combined with chronic fatigue and agonizing headaches. She had spent a small fortune on medical tests, but the army of specialists she consulted were convinced that her problems had no physical source.

Her third marriage was unraveling. Unemployment had become a way of life. Her weight was skyrocketing out of control. She had almost no friends. Even her grown children found it hard to be with her and made excuses not to be. Alone, obese, and suicidally depressed, she came to the counselor reluctantly and with little hope for change.

After only a few sessions it became apparent that there was something unusual about Edith's relationship with her older brother, Dennis. He had disappeared from her life years before, and no one seemed to know where he was. He was probably dead. The two had not seen each other in many years, but Edith spoke glowingly of how she loved Dennis. She was certain he regretted not seeing her. They had been very close, she gushed, truly the best of friends.

Dennis was six years her senior, so when she was nine, he was fifteen. He had been an exemplary older brother, she explained. He had "taken care" of her and really watched out for her. He had actually raised her, since their single mother worked, leaving them alone much of the time. He was her hero. He was the perfect big brother. Now, though, he was probably dead, and she was left to grieve him.

The sessions with the counselor were volatile. The seasoned counselor sensed that there was something more to Edith's relationship with her brother and wouldn't let the subject drop. Edith grew angry. She screamed. She resisted. She raged at the counselor and never ceased to be shrill and incensed. Eventually, wearied, her walls dismantled by the counselor's skilled probing, she dissolved into tears and let the vile truth pour out.

It turned out that Dennis had taken money from his friends in high school first to see his nine-year-old sister naked and then for her to give them oral sex. She did what they wanted, what her big brother wanted, but she hated every moment of every time it occurred. There was no father in the home. There was no protection. Dennis was the closest thing she had to a father, and she lived for his approval. And he used it.

Each time—and there were hundreds of times—that she stumbled gagging and retching into the bathroom, Dennis would storm out of the house, screaming at her not to be such a stupid baby. Their hardworking single mother was too fatigued to be concerned. The brother Edith idolized used her and held rejection over her head like a sword. So for years he "pimped her out" to any high school boy willing to pay.

There was shame, of course, but thankfully Edith was quick to unseat the lie that sought to hold her in that shame. The lie was that the shame was hers. It wasn't. It was Dennis'. It belonged to the boys who paid. When Edith unseated the lie of shame from its controlling throne, she began to be free. And quickly. In time the depression and the fatigue and the obesity and the headaches began to lose their grip.

This was only the beginning, though. Now she had to forgive. But how could she? She had nearly worshipped Dennis and given him everything a young girl had to give. Even years later she had convinced herself that he loved her, missed her, and grieved their separation as she did. Now she faced the truth. What kind of brother did such things? What kind of man—even at fifteen years old—watches his kid sister be violated by anyone willing to pay? Dennis was a dog. He was a pimp. He was a criminal. How she hated him!

Yet to be truly free, she had to forgive. Still, how could such a thing be forgiven?

Let me tell you one more story. Actually it is part of a story we already know.

I'm sure you remember Johnny from the previous chapter. You remember that he was seduced by an older woman when he was almost fifteen and then raped by her brother. You remember that they threatened to tell everyone about it. Johnny went on in life, remade himself, became successful, and never let anyone abuse him again. You also remember that a counselor had to help Johnny acknowledge that the rape even happened. In fact the counselor had to work hard just to get Johnny to use the word "rape." And then the shame had to be driven off with the liberating truth that the shame was not Johnny's to carry. It belonged to others. And the truth set him free from shame.

Now, though, he had to forgive. But how could he? It had been so vile, so nasty. He experienced such grace in driving off shame that he resented it when his counselor began talking about forgiveness. In fact the counselor's constant digging in this soil forced a return of nightmares that had gratefully ended years before. They returned on the wings of outrage, and it felt to Johnny like a setback. He had been free, he thought, and now the haunting began again. The nightmares took an awful turn toward the incident itself, though Johnny never actually dreamed the whole ordeal. He would awaken in sweat from the nightmarish feeling of being held, of being pinned down by strong hands and the weight of larger bodies. Always there was that sneering smile just above him.

While Johnny fought to forgive, someone near him fought the same battle. Meet Johnny's wife, Jenny.

She was a beautiful Christian woman. When she married Johnny, she had given herself to him fully. He had been so proud of her. She had a reputation as a talented woman with a deep devotional life and the gifts for adorning her husband's life with all that an exceptional woman can provide.

Yet she had spent years being shut out. Johnny's emotional distance had starved her of affection. She had been disappointed at first and then disillusioned. It ate into her relationship with God. It drained her of hope and the desire for her husband. Something was wrong with Johnny, but it all was hidden behind his bold, masculine exterior, the trappings of success, and his unshakable confidence in himself.

She feared the blowups. She despised the distance. She

resented the rejection. Making it all the worse was that Jenny came from a family background that was void of intimacy and seldom offered warmth and meaningful interaction. So her relationship with Johnny sucked the spirit from an inner reserve that was already desperately low in Jenny. She had hoped he would rescue her from the emotional barrenness she had known. But no, Johnny would never give of himself, never overflow with warmth and gentle love. He was not that man. He was not able.

Then came the revelation. Tearfully, Johnny told her of the rape and of all that he had suffered. He spoke of breakthroughs in counseling sessions and secrets shared with the counselor, a virtual stranger. While as a Christian she was grateful for any victory God won in a hurting life, the whole tale made her feel even further away from her husband, even more rejected and disillusioned. What Johnny told her was the most important truth of his life, and he had never even hinted of it to her all these years. Instead, so much shouting. So much distance. So much raging. Such horrible loneliness.

Now she was expected to forgive. She just didn't have it in her. Who did Johnny think he was to expect such a thing— after all he had stolen from her life?

These are hard stories to hear. Each of these people has been wronged. Each needs now to forgive both because it is the command of God and because it will set each of them free. Each person feels he or she has the right not to forgive. None of them, at this point in his or her story, knows how to forgive.

And what about you? You might not have experienced what these people have experienced, but do you have the same feelings? Have you been wronged in other ways? Are you tempted to exercise your right not to forgive? Is forgiveness a challenge for you as it is for these tortured souls? Answer these questions if you can. Now hold your answer before you as I show you a path out of the darkness.

THE THRONE OF LEGALISM

I'm going to say something that is hard to hear and that you have likely never heard before. Give me some time to explain before you are tempted to run from the truths I am about to share.

Here is the solid, but painful, truth we need to hear: unforgiveness is seated in legalism. Now, the legalism I'm talking about is not what you might think, particularly if you've gotten your meaning of the word from a religious life that emphasizes strict holiness. This is merely one manifestation of legalism. One may certainly be legalistic about clothing or makeup or some other type of behavior, but legalism itself is a far more profound issue.

Legalism is a worldview that sees all life's outcomes as a product of cause and effect, of if-then propositions. This reductionist philosophy initially comforts some for whom any randomness in the universe is distressing.

One may be legalistic about anything. Legalism is not, as some would have us think, confined to the religious community. Not in the least. One may be legalistic about nutrition, childbearing, personal finances, or money. In fact since legalism is a worldview, it can ooze into any area of our lives. Consider:

If you eat only vegetables, *then* you will not get cancer.

If you believe right, *then* you will get healed.

If you raise your children a certain way, *then* they will turn out "right."

Reducing life to such if-then "rules" makes it less fearful to face reality. We live in the assurance that life will work when we do the right things. If I hide myself in the right law, nothing bad will happen to me. I have a method, a system, a set of rules or laws to buffer me from the slings and arrows of life and from people who live outside "my law."

The problem, of course, is that when our so-called "laws" do not work, the injustice of it outrages my damaged emotions. Now, angry at the failed law, or at myself for not "rightly" keeping the law, or, most commonly, at God for not honoring the law, I am lacquered in unforgiveness. Bitterness coats my life inside and out. Why should I forgive a treacherous universe, the perverse people in my life, or the unjust God who will not play by the rules?

Our reasoning goes something like this: *I did the right thing. I homeschooled. My children should be shining examples of all that is good. Well, then why is my daughter on drugs? Where is the benefit of the law? Where is the God of the law?*

Or perhaps it goes something like this: *I believed and confessed and stood on the Word of God exactly as I was taught— not partially, but exactly as I was taught. Why does my husband have cancer? Is the law, then, not really the law? How can anyone explain a world like that? How can you live sanely in such an insane universe? I want the law to work. I want a God who honors His laws.*

What this means, of course, is that we want grace for our own sins and laws for everything else. All unforgiveness is seated in a sense of justice, and all justice is seated in law.

If justice doesn't work for everything all the time, every time, the universe is too scary a place to live in. We want scriptural promises to be immutable laws—laws, by the way, to which we can bind God Himself and demand an explanation or, even better, an apology.

This way of thinking can become a curse. Think about someone who completely believes, "Train up a child in the way he should go, and when he is old he will not depart from it" (Prov. 22:6). Then it goes wrong. He wants everyone to know, "I trained my child, and he did depart." Then he cries against heaven and as loudly as possible. Meanwhile the people down the street—alcoholics, mind you—have a son in the ministry. Where is the law? Where is God?

He becomes angry at the world and God. In fact he becomes angry at anyone who hurt and disappointed him. He becomes outraged. His devotion to justice has been betrayed.

Beyond that, and perhaps more importantly, his sense of injustice leaves him deeply insecure about trying again, let alone again and again. His devotion to the law may even motivate him to forgive, but he expects forgiveness to "work." When it doesn't, or doesn't work as he expected, his sense of injustice is actually deepened, and his ability to go on forgiving is mortally wounded.

I want to say it again: all unforgiveness is seated in legalism, a legalism that finds comfort and security in immutable cause-and-effect laws. Those laws are supposed to work, and when they don't, life becomes dangerous, and those who have held a legalistic worldview become unforgiving.

How, then, do we relate real life to Scripture? What about the verse mentioned earlier, "Train up a child in the way he should go, and when he is old he will not depart from it"? What about that?

I heard one famous Christian teacher on FamilyLife say, "You show me what's wrong with your teenager, and I'll show you what you did wrong as a parent."

That is one of the most destructive and condemnation-drenched statements ever laid on hurting parents. It is also seated in legalism. This view of parenting is an attempt to work backward from outcome to law. It is a sad and puny theology, which takes a good and encouraging verse of Scripture and turns it into a law with which we hope to bend God backward and bash the parents of wayward teens.

I have a question.

God raised Adam and Eve. God. In the Garden of Eden. Yet they still sinned. Did He raise them poorly? Did He make parental mistakes? Did He set a poor example, perhaps? Obviously not. Still Adam sinned. Was God responsible for Adam's sin? Blasphemy! You may be a great father, but let me assure you that what you are not is God Almighty. Your home may be a blessed place of Christian love, but it is not the Garden of Eden.

What do we, then, make of such a scripture? "Train up a child in the way he should go, and when he is old he will not depart from it" (Prov. 22:6). That's what it says, but it must not be read alone, separated from the rest of the Bible. It must be read in the light of balancing truths. We are all created just as Adam was, as free moral agents. Your children have a God-given and inalienable right to their own sins, and sometimes those sins have life-damaging consequences.

Therefore, what that verse actually means is this: "Raise up a child in the way he should go, and when he is grown, he will not depart from it...unless he does, just as Adam did. But if he does, God is still God, and there is still hope." I'm aware that this rendering of Proverbs 22:6 freaks legalists out. Nevertheless, in the light of the whole counsel of God, it's the right way to understand this verse.

To whatever extent you made mistakes with your prodigals, receive the grace of God, and pray for them to find that same grace. But do not get under the destructive legalistic bondage of taking all the blame. In the same way, when they turn out great, don't take too much credit. This is the way many promises of God must be read.

Take Luke 6:38, for another example: "Give, and it will be given to you. A good measure, pressed down, shaken together and running over, will be poured into your lap. For with the measure you use, it will be measured to you" (NIV).

That is a wonderful promise of God that encourages us to generosity and liberality in giving by assuring us that God will take care of us. However, if you turn it into an arm's-length, cash-on-the-barrelhead business arrangement with God, you suck all the joy out of it. You also turn it into a very human law with which you can impose your very human understanding of words such as *with the same measure*. If you give five dollars, and you expect five dollars in return, you may miss a far greater blessing that could be unleashed in your life if you would instead move in a joyful generosity far more reflective of God's character than a mere five-dollars-for-five-dollars business deal.

In addition, James 5:14 is clearly about developing a community of faith for healing and forgiveness: "Is anyone among you sick? Let them call the elders of the church to pray over them and anoint them with oil in the name of the Lord"

(NIV). On the other hand, if we read such verses apart from the promises of heaven and the totality of healing, we will turn that beautiful verse into a narrow-gauge law that will instead create an arrogant fellowship that can devolve into one of anger at failed laws and futile faith.

Keep in mind that all this sets us up for offense and unforgiveness since all such misunderstandings of Scripture plant demanding laws in our minds—laws that are not God's laws. It is when we hold others to similar laws that we find forgiveness difficult. We inflate a false sense of justice, inflate a universal truth of our own making, beyond the call to mercy and forgiveness. In doing so, we hold ourselves and others in the bondage of unforgiveness.

We see this devotion to an outsize justice even in the smallest of children. When Tommy yanks the toy out of Billy's hand, Billy screams about the wrong that has been done to him. He won't let it go; he cries and tells everyone who will listen how unfair and "just wrong" Tommy is. Young lives like these are open targets for the dominion of unforgiveness. Though he may not know it, the child can forgive the theft and the loss of the toy perhaps. But as he gets older, he finds the overarching injustice of life almost impossible to forgive. It is the principle, put in boyish terms, that outrages him: "Good boys ought not have toys stolen by bad boys" is the horror-stricken cry from the seat of justice.

Frankly this whole challenge of debilitating legalism can be harder for Christians than for others, and it is because their obligation to an inner "ought," an inner law, is usually very high. The same sense of law and eternal standards that moves them to live relatively holy lives in some areas can make them small and unforgiving in other areas of their lives. They don't

The Toxin of Unforgiveness

cuss and use foul language, because Scripture forbids it. Yet they do harbor deep bitterness toward Susie, who lied about them and gossiped, thus breaking "the law." So a person who intends to be a good and holy Christian can become an angry and unforgiving Christian, all because an unbiblical kind of legalism pervades his or her life.

THE THERAPY OF GRACE

The secret to dethroning the dominion of unforgiveness is grace. Receiving grace and granting grace demolishes legalism. The demand for justice is in effect a demand for law. The legalist wants a universe that runs by completely dependable laws, inviolable laws. Grace lets God run the universe His way.

The outcome of grace is mercy, and a life of mercy is forgiving and largely free of anger. The merciful do not hold their laws over others and expect freedom from the law for themselves. They want sinners healed, not destroyed.

Unfortunately it is this very clinging to exalted standards that causes the Christian ministry to often be haunted by envy and mercilessness. Many ministers live angry, unforgiving, and legalistic lives. This is especially true in religious subcultures that tend toward legalism historically and culturally. Believing in grace for salvation, these ministers often deny grace to one another. This is tragic, for shooting the wounded and humiliating the hurting creates a destructive, merciless environment that keeps ministers from seeking help. They hide their hurt, not daring to seek help, largely because they live in fear—a very reasonable fear—of being exposed and ridiculed.

59

The truth is that grace, in its broadest and deepest aspects, is the opposite of legalism. Grace embraces a loving God who is involved in the world but who does not micromanage a set of inviolable laws. In fact, grace teaches that God mercifully interrupts the punishment of the law as an outworking of His love.

Think about it. If you drop a teacup, gravity takes hold, and it breaks on the floor. This happens because it is "supposed to," because the outcome is determined by law. But what if God catches that teacup and keeps it from breaking? He loves you. He knows you value your teacup. He intervenes to show mercy, to interrupt the normal operation of laws for your good.

I've seen this mercy on God's part really enrage the legalists. A man who has become an alcoholic gets cirrhosis of the liver. This is law in motion. Too much alcohol leads to disease. Good. Law is working. The legalist is satisfied. Then God intervenes. He heals the man of cirrhosis and breaks the bondage of alcohol in his life. This enrages the legalist because law is interrupted. The law of love has trumped justice.

This attitude of hatred for interrupted law can even make legalists despise miracles. You think I'm exaggerating? Consider the most religious Jewish leaders of Jesus' day. Do you remember that they were incensed that Jesus was healing Gentiles? They were angry because Jesus was healing the wrong people, people who did not deserve it—the great unwashed. This was no way to run the universe, they believed. He should show mercy only to the right people so that their conception of law could be satisfied. Until they could see Jesus "come to His senses," those religious leaders of His day would rage against His healing of the undeserving.

What cuts through all this is that God is more concerned with people than with law. He wants us to be the same way. He wants us to stop pinning people to a fate determined by law and instead extend the mercy that sets both the offenders and us free. He wants us to pull down our inflated sense of justice—a justice we only expect for others, not for ourselves—and do as He does: be merciful so that all can be set right according to the standard of His love.

Let's look at how these truths played out in the lives of some of those whose stories we've learned.

JOHNNY AND FORGIVENESS

Johnny had been raped as a teenager and made himself a tough-hearted success to show the world who he was. He became a Christian, got help, and began to heal. He was making progress until forgiveness became the challenge.

The problem in forgiving for Johnny was anger. In locking up his own guilt and humiliating secrets, he also locked up a huge reservoir of anger. That anger kept oozing out under the door. It laced his relationships with an acidic undertaste. It showed up from time to time in confrontations but otherwise steeled itself into a hard detachment. He was not a screamer or a tantrum thrower. His rage was the more dangerous kind. It was cold rage.

Ultimately forgiveness for Johnny was a necessary contradiction. The wound now out in the open, his anger had to be discovered and expressed honestly. He had to see that his anger was normal under the circumstances. He had to get past his belief that as a Christian he was not allowed to feel anger, which is actually not a Christian truth at all.

Johnny's anger, locked away as it was, ate at him from the inside out. Brought out and processed, it became less of a bogeyman. Christians can be angry—in fact ought to be angry—at certain things. Johnny's suppressed anger was as destructive to him in some ways as the original outrage. His lifelong struggle with depression was anger held at bay, even turned inward.

Let's listen as the counselor helps Johnny deal with his anger by way of finding the path to forgiveness.

Counselor: Tell me, Johnny, when you think of these people, what they did to you, how do you feel?

Johnny: What do *you* think?

Counselor: I know what I think, but I would like for you to tell me. Are you in touch with your anger?

Johnny: I suppose.

Counselor: I suppose?

Johnny: What do you want me to say?

Counselor: Johnny, we've been here before. The truth. Don't tell me what you think I want to hear. I'm not looking for a "Christian" answer. I want you to answer right out of your gut.

Silence.

Counselor: You know it's OK for you to be angry.

Johnny: Of course I do.

Counselor: No, that's too flip. Do you know it? That day, for example, were you angry?

Johnny: Back then? That day it happened?

Counselor: Yes. Were you angry? Can you remember?

Johnny: You may not understand this, but I wasn't all that angry. I was humiliated and...

Counselor: And what?

Johnny: I was frightened they would tell. I didn't want anyone else to know. They threatened to tell, and I was absolutely terrified they would.

Counselor: And that kept you from being angry?

Johnny: No, I was angry too. It was just all mixed up. I was also angry at myself.

Counselor: For being caught in that situation?

Johnny: Yes. I shouldn't have been there at all. That's another reason I didn't tell anyone. I knew they would blame me. I felt like a stupid little jerk. I felt weak and angry because I couldn't defend myself. I was humiliated and frightened, and I wanted to die, and I wanted them to die. It was all very mixed up inside me.

Counselor: You couldn't make any sense of it, could you?

Johnny: No. It seemed to me that the only thing to do was just get past it. My family moved pretty soon after that, and I left it behind.

Counselor: Only you didn't, did you? Not really.

Johnny: No, I didn't.

Counselor: Now you can see that that young boy was a victim?

Johnny: I shouldn't have been there.

Counselor: OK, let's grant that. You did a wrong thing. A stupid, curious young boy thing, but it isn't in the same league with what they did. You can see that, can't you?

Johnny: Yes, I can.

Counselor: Then talk about all that anger, and fasten it where it belongs—on them. Tell me how angry you are. Put your arm around that boy, and tell me how angry you are that an adult, two adults, hurt him like that. Tell me. Go on, tell me the real anger.

Johnny: *Angry. Leaping to his feet. Striding about the office, weeping and shouting out his pent-up anger.* Angry? D*** them. God d*** them both to hell. How's that for anger. Hate? You cannot begin to understand how I hate them. D*** them both to hell.

Counselor: You know it's all right for you to say that.

Johnny: It is? Well, I said it. You wanted the real answer, and you got it. *Now flushed with anger. Shouting again and cursing. Now weeping. Anger rising in his voice as he continues to curse.*

Counselor: Probably. But you really want to make that decision?

Johnny: What difference does that make? I don't get to decide. You asked me how I felt, and I told you.

Counselor: Yes, but what if God offered you the choice? You can decide or let Him decide. Would you take the decision out of God's hands to send those people to hell or leave it with Him? Are you willing for God to decide their judgment?

Johnny: I guess so *(with a shrug).*

Counselor: You guess so? This is important, Johnny. This is so important a part of healing that you cannot answer, "I guess so." Are you willing for God to decide?

Johnny: *His face in his hands. Weeping softly.* Yes, I'm probably going to hell myself. Let God decide.

Counselor: Oh, Johnny, that's huge. Don't you see when you let go of them, they have no more hold on you? Letting go of the "hell question" is the first step to forgiveness.

Johnny: Theirs or mine?

Counselor: Both, Johnny. Both.

JENNY AND FORGIVENESS

While Johnny was just beginning to find the grace to forgive, his wife, Jenny, was in the thick of her own battle. The truth is that the agony of the offended is very real. *Shall I forgive? If I do, will I just get hurt again? Can this person change? Does my forgiveness help this person change?* These and a thousand other questions haunt the hurting. The problem is that the answers are all hidden in an as yet unrevealed future.

I do not know—in fact, I cannot know—whether the person who has wronged me will change. Who can predict that? Yet this is what the offended fear: being suckers, being hurt over and over again while the world mocks them as being too soft, too quick to let wrongs go. That is the leap of faith Jenny had to take as she pursued the therapy of forgiveness with her counselor. Emotional risk is always hardest for the emotionally wounded.

It was particularly hard for Jenny. A lifetime of struggling to get past the rejection she experienced in her parents' home had left her emotionally damaged. Her marriage had been a roller-coaster search for wholeness. Johnny's secrets, distance, and seething anger combined with Jenny's fear of intimacy had constructed near impregnable walls between them.

Though Jenny worked with her counselor to make huge strides in dealing with her own fear of intimacy, Johnny seemed to work against her. Then came that last blowup, which brought Jenny's wonderful progress toward healing to a screeching halt. "I cannot do this anymore," she told herself. "I cannot risk forgiving. I cannot let myself love again."

She could not, absolutely could not—but she did. Her anger was real, and she vented it. There were some pretty explosive times, but she watched and waited. She also tested Johnny. As it turned out, he had changed. A healing had begun. Repentance and forgiveness had begun their work. Jenny, though, had to be sure. She consciously and subconsciously pushed every button Johnny had. She watched him like a hawk for any of the old emotional habits. No withdrawing. No angry rebuttal. No defense. No prideful wall descending around him. She took it right to the limit. Would he last? Would his apparent changes prove to be enduring and real?

Jenny also had to learn a new and challenging marital skill: confrontation. This did not come easily for her. My guess is it was a new and not all that appealing development for Johnny as well. She had to start confronting Johnny consistently, whenever his old emotional habits of retreat and isolation would rear their heads. She had to do this not once but repeatedly, until these behaviors gradually disappeared entirely from view. It was a strenuous and difficult season for them both, but the payoff in honesty and increased intimacy was well worth the effort.

There were years of counseling. Both Johnny and Jenny did hard emotional work. They fought fierce battles with old wounds and destructive emotional habits. Nothing came easily, but it came. In time Jenny's love renewed and forgiveness, true forgiveness, came. Jenny's therapy of forgiveness was an inner work, a deep work of the Wonderful Counselor, much more than just human counseling. A beautiful rebirth of love followed. It was a painful and risky inner process, but Jenny faced it heroically.

The therapy of integration was the challenge that followed forgiveness. Again, because of her exceptional inner devotional life, Jenny processed a fresh look at integration largely alone with the Wonderful Counselor. The world she had worked very hard throughout her life to bring to a comprehensive whole had ripped open at the seams. To integrate new elements, her world had to dilate dangerously. How far could it stretch to integrate and not disintegrate?

What did God working "all things" together mean to Jenny? Could the revelations of Johnny's past be added into her world? What about his failings? Stretched to the breaking point, Jenny basically started over to integrate fresh levels of painful disillusionment and disappointment. Gradually she began to make sense of it all. Then connecting lines had to be drawn to reach heretofore unexplored extremity. Just when she had gotten "all things" in her life to work together, new things had to be reckoned with. The Wonderful Counselor helped her with a grace she had never known.

That "all things work together for good" became real for Johnny and Jenny in very visible and powerful ways. What they went through was excruciating. It was "the valley of the shadow" (Ps. 23:4). They had previously made the decision, for their children and all the others in their world, to absorb their pain privately. That fateful choice filled their home with pain. Both of them walked alone in "the valley of the shadow" during that time. Both found themselves without the strength to go on. Then they discovered a presence in the wilderness. They both discovered the Wonderful Counselor in that secret agony. Jenny particularly processed her grief with the Wonderful Counselor. Johnny discovered more intimacy with God born of pain and desperation. Then, ultimately, they rediscovered each other.

Alone at first, agonizingly alone, they kept working out their pain with their counselor. "What will this accomplish?" they often wondered aloud. Can Johnny hang in there? So many husbands bail out on the process and cut and run. There was fear. There were lonely nights. Always there were rivers of tears. Still they kept walking. They kept dealing with their pain and disappointments. In long, hard talks, they cleared the air. It was not easy. They had to walk out their commitments. There was often pain in every conversation, in every word. Still they broke down walls that they had once refused to acknowledge. Now, brick by brick, they tore down the walls they had built. Always, courageously, they kept walking toward healing.

Then something began to happen in "the valley of the shadow." Slowly love was reborn. When the walls came down, intimacy was reborn. The veil was torn away. Johnny and Jenny entered into a new place. Together. Now "the valley of the shadow" became a place of intimacy. They encountered the Wonderful Counselor and each other. He anointed their heads with oil. He prepared a table before them in their former wilderness. Their cups actually did run over. There was new wine in a new place. Weeping endured for the night, yes, but joy came in the morning. Eventually shame and guilt and grief and pain yielded to a new work of the Spirit: intimacy. Johnny and Jenny found a new level of honesty, the ability to talk about anything, absolutely anything. They did not have to hide their emotions for fear of each other.

Jenny discovered a man who could listen, who could allow her to hurt without pulling away. Johnny came out from behind a lifetime of impregnable walls. He was then able to discover a strong, mature woman who saw him, really saw him, and forgave the failings, embraced the past, and found faith for the future. After all the torturous years, they found each other in the presence of the Wonderful Counselor.

EDITH AND FORGIVENESS

You remember the horrific story of Edith, I'm sure. Pimped out at nine years of age by her older brother, she then hid the memory for years. It was never suppressed or forgotten. The horrible story was never told to anyone else until she told the counselor, but she remembered it every day of her life. Only in counseling, though, was she able to process what her brother had done.

Forgiveness, always a huge issue for the bitterly wounded, is complicated even further when the offender is absent or likely deceased. This is because of the fantasy views of forgiveness most people hold. They envision some beautiful moment of "closure" where their offenders can confess and plead for forgiveness. They see themselves in almost Christlike grace wiping the sin away. Always there is a grand, emotional reunion.

This fantasy becomes impossible when the offender is dead. In this case people often imagine that forgiveness is also impossible. The counselor has to help them understand that the offender is not at all necessary to their therapy of forgiveness. If the offending party were alive, it would not matter or change a thing. Forgiveness happens solely in the offended.

I do not need a response from my tormentors to forgive. Their lack of response cannot hinder me. I can forgive whether the offending person even knows about my need to forgive, asks for it, accepts it, or rejects it. I can forgive the living, the dead, those whom I will never see again, and for that matter those whose names I do not know but who have nonetheless wounded me. The people I forgive may not want my forgiveness, know I have granted it, know who I am, or ever repent and change. Forgiveness is mine alone to grant, and the healing it catalyzes is in me alone.

As Edith painfully worked her way through the therapy of forgiveness, she came to see two liberating and healing truths. First, forgiving her brother's horrendous abuse of her did not excuse it or minimize its devastating effects on her life. Forgiving him ended his final hold on her. By forgiving him, he could hurt her no more. His actions severely damaged her emotions, but her forgiveness began her healing.

Second, she realized that she could forgive her brother even though he was probably dead. This was crucial to her healing. If we cannot forgive the dead, then the dead carry the key to our inner healing to the grave with them. God forbid.

Edith forgave, forgave fully, and was set free. She did not let any legalistic thinking about her brother's deeds keep her from completely absolving him and, more importantly, completely releasing herself from the prison of unforgiveness. She is liberated now, having lived through what would have debilitated most people for their entire lives.

DEVON AND FORGIVENESS

You remember Devon, I'm sure. In a nasty divorce, he lost the ranch his father had built. He ended up living in a dingy townhouse in a seedy town not too far from where his ex-wife lived on Devon's ranch with her lawyer lover.

Devon's sense of law worked against him at first. "How am I supposed to forgive this?" he wailed loudly and often. "This should never have happened. I had witnesses who spoke to my character and proved that she was adulterous. What kind of justice is this? The court ordered us to sell the ranch, my family's ranch, and split the proceeds. She bought me out. The court ordered that too. Now she shacks up there with her lawyer. How is that supposed to happen? Well, it shouldn't, so how am I supposed to forgive that?"

In other words, Devon's sense of what should or could be forgiven was tied to what should and should not have happened in a just universe. *There are rules, aren't there? A decent guy just ought not to lose the family ranch to a conniving woman and her shyster lawyer. I lived a good life. I never cheated on her. She cheated on me. Rules are rules. Aren't they? Right is right. Isn't it?*

The poison of unforgiveness is lethal. It is an infection that can only be cured by the medicinal application of its opposite. That sounds strange, doesn't it? Imagine if a physician told you the cure for pneumonia was to take some "un-pneumonia," and the worse your case of pneumonia became, the more "un-pneumonia" you would need. The only problem is that the medicine is hard to take, and the more you need, the harder it is to take.

The problem with forgiveness is exactly that. The cure, the only cure, for unforgiveness is forgiveness. That is the forgiveness conundrum. Forgiveness is only possible when there is an offense, a wound, and the greater the wound, the more "medicine" needed. It just seems wrong, really wrong, that someone made me sick, and I have to take the medicine. The wound is outrage enough. The medicine seems to be salt in the wound. The cure seems worse than the curse.

In other words, forgiveness is not a philosophy of life. It's a practice, and a practice that can only be performed in response to a wound. The greater the wound, the more medicine needed, but the more medicine needed, the less I want to swallow it. Simply put, one cannot forgive until there is something to forgive. The more outrageous that "something" is, the harder it is to forgive.

How much medicine does it take to get well? This is not a frivolous question. Peter asked it in this way: "Lord, how many teaspoons of forgiveness must I take because of what someone else does to me? Will seven teaspoons heal me?" (See Matthew 18:21.)

Jesus' answer is hard to hear. The more you're wounded, the more medicine you need. Seventy teaspoons? Yes. Some multiple of that? Yes. One's resistance to forgiving is not just relative to the depth of the wound. It is magnified by one's internal sense of justice, the way things ought to be in the universe. That is actually blaming God.

The formula for computing the damage done to an unforgiving soul is this: the perceived depth of the wound multiplied by the sense of justice inside the aggrieved party equals the resistance to the "medicine" of forgiveness. The medicine must therefore equal or exceed the resistance. That's it.

This is what Devon wanted to know. He actually had two questions: How can this happen? And how do I live with this? The first question is actually an accusation. What Devon meant was, How can a good God let this happen, especially to me? The counselor had to start there.

Counselor: Let me ask you a question: Is this a just universe?

Devon: No, I guess not. Not always. But there ought to be some justice.

Counselor: When?

Devon: What? What does that even mean? Do you realize you ask really irritating questions?

Counselor: So I've been told. Let me ask it another way. You said there ought to be some justice. What if I said there cannot be *some*, but there can be *total* justice? That all accounts ought to be settled? That every evil deed should be punished and justice meted out to all offenders, offenders such as your ex-wife and her lawyer? How does that sound?

Devon: OK. OK, I'm good with that. Not *some* justice but *total* justice. Good! I like that better.

Counselor: Are you sure? I mean, think now. All offenders. What about your offenses?

Devon: *Angry now.* I never stole anybody's ranch.

Counselor: No, but you've done some bad stuff. Right? Your bad stuff may not be as wicked as their bad stuff, but still... Well, you see where I'm headed, right?

Devon: I'm a Christian.

Counselor: What's that got to do with justice?

Devon: Grace! I mean, what about forgiveness? That's what everybody preaches, isn't it? Your sins are under the blood. That's what my preacher says.

Counselor: Does grace just cancel out justice?

Devon: You tell me.

Counselor: No. You tell me.

Devon: Yes. All right. Yes. The grace of God cancels out justice in my life. Isn't that right? I thought that's what the Bible says. Is that right or not?

Counselor: Yes, I believe it is right. In other words, because of God's grace, you're not going to get what you deserve for your bad stuff.

Devon: That's what I understand all these preachers are saying.

Counselor: Me too. That's what I understand. But here's my question: It sounds as if you don't want to get what you deserve, but you want your ex-wife and that lawyer to get what's coming to them. Is that right?

Devon: I see what you're saying, but...

Counselor: But what?

Devon: What do I have to do with that? Their forgiveness isn't in my hands, is it? God forgave me. Let Him forgive them.

Counselor: What if something you are doing right now were to cancel out God's grace in your life? What if all that bad stuff could suddenly just come back on you?

Devon: Can that happen?

Counselor: Do you ever pray the Lord's Prayer?

Devon: A lot. All the time.

Counselor: Do you? Do you recognize this line: "Forgive us our trespasses, as we forgive those who trespass against us"?[1] Ever say that part?

Devon: *Looking stunned.* Does it work like that?

Counselor: I don't know, does it?

Devon: I hate it when you do that, ask me right back like that. I really hate that, and you do it all the time.

Counselor: Please forgive me.

Devon: Of course. I was just...

Counselor: No. Stop. I mean, please forgive me.

Devon: OK. I didn't mean to make a big deal...

Counselor: Are you listening to me? Please forgive me.

Devon: What?

Counselor: Isn't that what you said to God?

Devon: Yes.

Counselor: Now I'm saying it to you.

Devon: OK.

Counselor: According to what the Lord's Prayer says, do you think God wants you to forgive me?

Devon: *Angry again.* Well, I think stealing a d*** ranch is just a little bit different, don't you?

Counselor: Different in what way?

Devon: Well, it's a little bit worse, wouldn't you say?

Counselor: Yes, I'd say it is. But isn't forgiveness the answer for big stuff just as for little stuff? I mean, maybe just more of it. Bigger sin needs bigger forgiveness. Does that seem right?

Devon: I see what you're saying. But they haven't asked me. They will never ask me.

Counselor: Where is that in the Lord's Prayer?

Devon: You're saying I should forgive them whether they ask or not.

Counselor: No. You said it. You said you pray it all the time.

Devon: Just like that? I forgive them? Just like that? You make it sound mighty easy. Adultery. Stealing my ranch that's been in my family for generations. Could you do that? Could you forgive that? Tell me the truth.

Counselor: No.

Devon: But you expect me to, right? Just let them off the hook and wash my hands of it, right?

Counselor: No. I expect Jesus to. You decide to go the way of forgiveness, and He will do it through you. Here's the thing, though: It will not let them off the hook. You don't get to decide that. It lets you off the hook. You're here because your soul needs healing. You told me in a previous session that you're sick of being like this. Well, "like this" is bitter and unforgiving and sad. Forgiving them won't heal them, but it will heal you.

Devon looked as if he had been slapped. His eyes widened. He said nothing for a long time. The counselor waited. This couldn't be hurried.

Devon: I'm sick of being like this.

Counselor: I know. It's time to start getting well, don't you think?

Devon: I know I can't go on like this much longer.

Counselor: You're right, you can't go on like this much longer. It will get worse.

Devon: *Beginning to cry.* Oh, God, help me.

Counselor: He will. He's ready if you are.

Devon: I've got to get past this.

Counselor: Let's start this way: let's pray the Lord's Prayer together.

Devon's journey into wholeness began right there, right then. He knew it wasn't going to be easy, but he took that first step courageously, and in fact his journey into wholeness, a joyful and liberating wholeness, was easier and faster and more complete than he—or that counselor—ever imagined it would be.

In all these stories, glorious healing came once the courageous moment of facing the truth occurred. Yet even once the truth had been faced, often the issue of legalism had to be confronted. Devon only got free when he stopped being offended with the existence of loss and injustice in the universe. Jenny began to heal when she stopped rigidly holding Johnny to laws of expectation she had come to embrace. And Johnny found the beginnings of wholeness when he left the question of punishment in the hands of God and humbly sought mercy for his failures.

These are tender, inspiring stories of healing. Yet let us never forget the healing process: These dear people had to face the truth courageously. They had to acknowledge their pain. They had to let go of their legalistic worldview, leave judgment to God, and forgive their offenders. Ultimately they had to embrace mercy and do the hard homework of welcoming healing in their souls.

I hope you will take a long, serious look into these stories and see how they can reflect truth into your life.

- How are you hiding from truth?

- What have you yet to acknowledge?

- What emotions about the wrongs done to you do you need to surface?

- How do you need to let go of legalism and give yourself to mercy so you can be free?

- Finally, how is the Wonderful Counselor trying to lead you in paths of healing and wholeness?

These may be the most important questions for your life.

JOHNNY—AGAIN

I want to close this chapter on forgiveness with a final, tender dialogue between Johnny and his counselor. I trust it will help you. I'm eager to draw all the victory I can from Johnny's painful story. Through this may the enemy of our souls be defeated by the Wonderful Counselor in His great work in our lives.

Johnny: You know, when I think about how I hurt Jenny and sinned against her, there's one verse of Scripture that haunts me.

Counselor: Of course there is. I even know what it is.

Johnny: You do?

Counselor: Yes. You are a Christian believer. You sinned. Now you're afraid of having committed the unpardonable sin.

Johnny: You sound a little flip about it. It is a terrifying verse. I heard a famous preacher say that if you sin deliberately after being filled with God's Spirit, you cannot be forgiven.

Counselor: Sometimes famous preachers say stupid things. Fame is no safeguard against stupidity.

Johnny: My sins were deliberate.

Counselor: All sin is deliberate. Nobody sins by accident.

Johnny: Well, what about it then? Can a person be forgiven for deliberate sins after becoming a Spirit-filled believer?

Counselor: If God will not forgive Spirit-filled Christians who sin, hell will be packed. I'm not making light of what you did. Those phone calls to that nasty porn service were sinful. They hurt your wife, they hurt your family, and they hurt your reputation at your company, but they were not the unforgivable sin.

Johnny: Are you sure?

Counselor: You just extended forgiveness to two people who committed an atrocity against a child. Can God, then, not forgive a hurting, emotionally damaged Christian who makes some phone calls? Are you more forgiving than God is? Or was your sin worse than theirs?

Johnny: But they were not Christians. I was.

Counselor: In other words, only unbelievers can be forgiven for their sins? If that is true, I don't see the point in becoming a Christian.

Johnny: Well, what is the unforgivable sin?

Counselor: One thing I know: you haven't committed it, or you wouldn't even want God's forgiveness. The unforgivable sin is to blaspheme the Holy Spirit for the intentional purpose of turning others against God. It is the utter cauterization of the soul in order to drag others away from Jesus. Are you repentant?

Johnny: Yes, I truly am.

Counselor: Are you willing to ask God for His forgiveness and believe by faith?

Johnny: My faith is pretty weak and wounded right now.

Counselor: Weak and wounded faith works just fine.

Johnny: Yes, I want God's forgiveness.

Counselor: Then receive it and thank Him for it.

Johnny: *Weeping now.* Thank You, God. Thank You for forgiving me.

Counselor: Jenny has forgiven you also, hasn't she?

Johnny: Yes. It's a miracle.

Counselor: Yes, it is a miracle, but she did. Your wife has forgiven you, and God has forgiven you. We have to settle this now. If you cannot receive and accept God's forgiveness, you cannot get on with your healing. Believe God, or believe your own guilt. That is the choice you have to make. Healing is where you want to go. Guilt and condemnation stand in your way. Think back. Think back to how we dealt with shame from that incident in your youth. Look how far we've come. What you did was wrong. I'm not excusing it.

You hurt your wife badly. You hurt a lot of people. Now what do we do with that?

Johnny: I feel disqualified.

Counselor: By what you did? Disqualified from leadership as a Christian?

Johnny: Yes.

Counselor: You are.

Johnny: What?

Counselor: You are disqualified. If sin disqualifies people from leadership, then you're disqualified.

Johnny: Is that supposed to be comforting?

Counselor: It's not my goal to comfort you. It's my goal to help you become a whole person, fulfilling your calling.

Johnny: But you think I'm disqualified?

Counselor: You are disqualified. But who is qualified if sin disqualifies people from Christian leadership? No one is. God doesn't use people in leadership because they are sinless. He uses them because He is a God of grace. He has a purpose for you, and He is working a miracle of healing in you to get all the gunk out of your gears, stuff going all the way back to your youth, so that you can get on with what He has called you to do. Johnny, you think others in leadership are perfect. They are not. And you're not. Perfection is not wholeness. Wholeness is our goal, isn't it?

Johnny: Yes.

Counselor: No, not so easily as that. I'm asking you, Is wholeness what you want?

Johnny: Yes, wholeness is what I want.

Counselor: If it is, and you tell me it is, then you have to see both the faces of forgiveness. You must acknowledge and accept them—both of them. You must accept God's forgiveness and then, forgiven, you must forgive.

Johnny: I want that. Truly I do, but I just cannot seem to get there. How? How do I get there? You're always talking about therapy. Is there a therapy for that?

Counselor: Yes, it's called grace. The therapy of grace.

The evil throne of justice is my own lust for inflated justice. A wrong has been done. More specifically, a wrong has been done to me. A toxin, a river of unforgiving bitterness, flows out of that throne because I have believed a lie. That lie is this: if I forgive someone, the person will escape justice. If I want the person to be judged more than I want myself to be healed, I will never be healed. Never. It is as simple as that.

The lie that gives unforgiveness its toxic power is that if I forgive, the person goes free. The truth that heals me is that if I forgive, I go free. As long as I cling to the hope of the person's condemnation, I actually seal my own. Here is the truth: My forgiveness does nothing for those I forgive. It heals me.

Biblical counseling for unforgiveness finds its greatest resource in the Lord's Prayer and the verses that follow it, found in Matthew 6:14–15. This is the truth that heals my unforgiving heart.

> Our Father in heaven, hallowed be your name, your kingdom come, your will be done, on earth as it is in heaven. Give us today our daily bread. And forgive us our debts, as we also have forgiven our debtors. And lead us not into temptation, but deliver us from the evil one.

For if you forgive other people when they sin against you, your heavenly Father will also forgive you. But if you do not forgive others their sins, your Father will not forgive your sins.

—MATTHEW 6:9–15, NIV

Chapter 4

THE TOXIN OF REJECTION

TOXIN	THRONE	THERAPY	GOAL
Rejection	Doubt	Trust	Acceptance

HAVING DROPPED OUT of college and forfeited a full-tuition gymnastics scholarship and a possible berth on the Olympic team, Janet plunged into depression. She had no idea why she left school or why her depression deepened so dangerously. She explained to the counselor that the only thing she knew for sure was that she would never do gymnastics again as long as she lived. She also made it clear—and she was nearly hysterical as she did—that if her parents could not accept her decision about this, she couldn't care less and may never see them again.

She had begun gymnastics on her own. It was her idea. At least it was her idea insofar as she was allowed to have any ideas of her own. Her parents were controlling—obsessively controlling, in fact. When she showed an early interest in gymnastics and then displayed an amazing talent for it, they dove in headlong. Coaches and private lessons were only the beginning. The entire family was completely absorbed. They attended every meet. Her mother even watched every lesson.

Janet appreciated the devotion and the sacrifice. She knew her parents were not wealthy people. She also knew that she should be grateful. Many of her friends longed for parents who took an interest in their activities. Yet at a certain point, two things began to haunt Janet.

First, she was not sure if her parents were really about her or were about her successes. Second, she knew she wanted out of gymnastics, but she couldn't figure out how to tell them. All the money and time and lessons and gym meets— all of it!—what about all that? It was like being caught up in a lie that just got bigger and bigger until you couldn't get out of it and you couldn't think of who to tell.

Two serious bouts with anorexia later, her hair was falling out and her hands shook uncontrollably when she entered the gym. When she showed up on her parents' doorstep, baggage in hand, she was ready for counseling. What she was facing was her deep fear of rejection. Janet had been the perfect child. Obedient, submissive, intelligent, and well-mannered. The perfect child. Now what?

The Throne of Doubt

Rejection is seated in doubt. These doubts are both inflicted and inborn. It is absolutely certain that some children are predisposed to doubt the loving and nurturing voices around them. As adults those who are so predisposed need healing as well as those whose doubts are caused by wounding experiences.

Rejection is far more than simply being left out of a club or being unchosen on the playground. It is a deep-tissue conviction of being superfluous in the universe. More than being just uncared for by some particular person or group, rejection is an emotional wound deep within that leaves a gaping hole, a sense of being unloved, unlovable, and unwanted. Rejection is a question, not a statement, and that question is, What is wrong with me?

Two voices war inside our emotions. One says, "I am an accepted person, beloved of my parents and God, and I belong in the universe." Another voice says, "No one really loves me. My family may pretend to, my friends are in it for the fun, and God...I seriously doubt, I mean, I *seriously* doubt He loves me."

That is actually the crux of the matter. The negative voice (voice number two) doubts the positive inner assurance of acceptance. In fact it doubts, seriously doubts, the correlating evidence of acceptance life can produce. The mystery of *why* I am rejected is haunting! The emotionally wounded may well spend their entire lives pondering the disquieting question of *why*. The *who* is basically anyone. It can even become a *what*: the universe itself somehow rejects me. What is wrong with me?

In fact that depressing question can lead them into deeply unbalanced responses to minor perceived rejections that may very well be imagined. They can see rejection in everything. The voice of doubt screams in their ear at every incident. Religious teaching that speaks of a loving and accepting God is doubted. Avowals by lovers, spouses, and family members are tentatively held as "maybes" at best, then doubted immediately at the first "proof" that their love and acceptance were insincere.

Somehow this person's trust mechanism is damaged, perhaps by childhood experiences and relational disappointments. Others are simply born with defective trust mechanisms. Either way, they need healing. The therapy of trust is a crucial key to healing rejection.

As strange as it may sound, sexual trauma is also a form of rejection, a brutal, humiliating form. In sexual trauma personhood is rejected and the victim is horribly objectified—a thing to be used, not a person to be related to, accepted, and loved.

Another form of rejection is control. "Stage parents," for example, who push their children into sports or performance, actually pour rejection on the child. The sense of being loved or accepted only for a willingness to meet expectations is rejection. The more controlling the parents, the more deep-seated the sense of rejection. Some children act out from a sense of rebellion. *Since you have rejected me, I reject you, your rules, your demands, your control, everything you are and stand for.* This is preemptive rejection. Others acquiesce in hopes of finally being accepted.

Doubt: The Seat of Rejection

Look again at the chart in the first section. Rejection is a toxin that is always lethal but frequently not the result of trauma. Like all the emotional toxins described in this book, rejection is seated in a throne of power, a dominion, if you will, and that dominion is doubt. Doubt derives its power from a lie, and that lie is, *Something is wrong with and unlovable about me.*

Unable to feel love or perhaps never having felt it, I doubt, *profoundly* doubt, that I can be loved. That doubt, fed by a satanic lie, becomes the opportunistic beast living just outside the door, waiting for one more proof that I am unlovable. When that proof comes, the beast will pounce, and the wound erupts again. Sometimes that eruption is explosive. More often it is a quiet poison, oozing a corruption that eats away at faith. There, lie says, there is more proof: see, you are not loved.

THE THERAPY OF TRUST

If the toxin of rejection is empowered by a lie, the antidote must be a truth, *the truth*. Ephesians 1:5–6 (NIV) is the answer, and it is the beginning of all healing for rejection:

> He predestined us for adoption to sonship through Jesus Christ, in accordance with his pleasure and will—to the praise of his glorious grace, which he has freely given us in the One he loves.

I am accepted. By whom? God, of course. If God has chosen me, accepted me, and adopted me, who can reject me?

The slow, long-term wound of rejection is not usually some violent trauma but rather a lifetime of pinpricks. Therefore, healing will most often come by an elongated process of learning to trust, not humanity but Jesus. Our confidence in humans, even the best of them, must always be tempered by the reality that none of us are perfect. Every human will eventually do something that will disappoint someone else. Wounded humanity wounds wounded humanity.

"I cannot believe he did that" is the mantra of the naive. People, even the finest people whom we love the most, are fully capable of doing stupid, disappointing, even sinful things. We all must live with that reality. It is when life pounds that into you, when your family is cold and unloving, when you are never chosen to be on anybody's team, when you are never invited to birthday parties, when all that piles up over a lifetime that the whole thing tilts. Our understanding of the frailty of humanity becomes an unbalanced, bitter doubt. Then we are easy prey for the lie that something, something awful that we cannot see, is wrong with us and keeps us from ever being really loved.

The healing process, the therapy for rejection, is the constant, regular application of the balm of Gilead, and that soothing, healing salve is Ephesians 1:5–6. Being counseled back to balance when suffering from rejection is coming to see that trust, the basis of relational trust, lies in trusting the One who chose me, accepted me, and adopted me. I can then allow my trust of others to come into a healthy balance. Because I learn to lean back into the arms of God, I can even begin to trust others again, in a balanced way. The One, the only One, worthy of my full trust is God. I know I can never expect any other to be as perfect as He is, but I can now live free of the bitter toxin of constant, angry rejection. It will not happen in a day, but then neither did the wound to my emotions.

ACCEPTANCE: THE FRUIT OF TRUST

Restored trust is not reconstructed naivete. Pollyanna platitudes and the denial of the carnal ability of others to act destructively is *not* wholeness. It is just another kind of emotional damage. A restored trust mechanism does not mean that we let sex offenders babysit or we commit our own emotional well-being into the hands of emotionally damaged relatives.

A restored trust mechanism affords the inner health to know several things.

I am accepted by God, just as Ephesians 1:6 teaches: "to the praise of the glory of His grace, by which He made us accepted in the Beloved."

1. When my trust mechanism is healed, I can doubt my doubts on this account. I can trust the Scriptures. I can trust the character of God. God will not—in fact, cannot—lie to me. I am accepted by God.

2. I am acceptable. There is no sign on my back that everyone else can see and that I alone cannot. There is no mysterious flaw in me from birth. I am strangely and wonderfully made, and God does not find me unacceptable. Furthermore, nothing anyone else can do or ever has done can render me unacceptable. What others do may make them unacceptable, yet they leave no fingerprints on me. None. No matter what. No shameful assault on my body makes me, my mind, my spirit, or my body unacceptable. That which is done to me does not make me unacceptable.

3. No one can truly reject someone God has accepted. People simply do not have that power or authority. Their words cannot cancel His word. Their judgments against me are useless in the face of His grace and acceptance. Their rejection has no effect on my acceptance. It is in them alone and is the manifest proof of their woundedness.

4. If no one has the authority to reject me, that includes me. I must be accepted in my own eyes. I see myself as accepted, acceptable, and beloved of God. I refuse to arrogantly reject myself, one whom God has accepted. He is a wiser, better, holier, more discerning judge than I am. He says I am accepted, and I accept His decision.

5. I accept my whole life and self. My history is mine. I do not have to deny it or wall it off or seal it up because though it is mine, it has no power to define me as unacceptable. I embrace the story of my life and God's redemptive purpose in it. All of my life. I am a whole person able to see my whole life, warts, hurts, damage, and failures included and still know that by grace I am accepted.

SUSAN'S STORY

Susan's parents were alcoholics. Her father was a "functioning alcoholic"—fairly successful in business while never being altogether sober. He drank himself to sleep every night, drank at lunch, drank after calls, before dinner, after dinner, in fact drank constantly. He was never violent with Susan. He was absent, emotionally absent, drunk, and cold. The drunken bouts of screaming were not with Susan but with her mother.

If her father's alcoholism was the constant, cold reality of their home, her mother's binges were frequent explosions. Susan's father was the passive drunk, never sober, never loud or violent, and never really present. Her mother was frequently drunk and dangerous when drunk, and more often than not Susan was her first target. One night Susan's mother threatened her with a butcher knife. Another time she attacked Susan with a pair of scissors. Locked in her bathroom, Susan wept in terror, enduring once again her mother's alcohol-fueled rages.

She married young. He was a dependable, solid citizen. Hers was the ideal suburban life. She had a nice house, a successful husband, and a membership at the local fitness center, where she worked out. Frequently. She began to run. Every day. Miles at a time. Eventually this was not enough to lose the weight she wanted. She exercised more and ate less. In fact she ate less and less every day.

Her husband noticed. Then he became concerned. Then he grew truly frightened. Susan began to resent his "constant nagging." They argued bitterly. Occasionally at first, then daily. *Why was he being so stupid about this? Why was everyone around her being so stupid?* Two hospitalizations later and after a tongue-lashing from her family physician, Susan reluctantly agreed to see the counselor. She had no idea why. She only conceded to shut everyone up. There was nothing wrong. She was adamant about that. There was nothing wrong with her, and she told her counselor so at her first visit.

Counselor: Then why are you here?

Susan: I have no idea, absolutely no idea.

Counselor: What do they think is wrong, your husband and the others?

Susan: I am not an anorexic. I don't care what they say.

A month later, another hospitalization later, a threatened divorce later, Susan was finally ready to admit to anorexia. Calling it what it was, anorexia, was heroic. Just like Johnny and Edith, Susan had to face the truth, then name the truth, which at last she did. And as it was for Johnny, this step was just the beginning of her journey.

Her anorexia was not really about food. It was about control. Working with the counselor, she began to see that her longing to escape her disordered childhood had led to an obsessive need for control. The chaos in which she grew up fueled her determination for control. Her father would not control her ever again. Neither would her mother's rages. She would. She alone.

She had stubbornly refused to move twice in her marriage, both times damaging her husband's career and very nearly destroying her marriage. Anything new, any uncertainty, would upset her inordinately. Finally her life became an obsession with exercise and a starvation diet. Her entire wardrobe became nothing but workout clothes. Her relationships almost completely disappeared.

By the time she agreed to see the counselor, she not only would not move, but all she had left was an ever-shrinking lifestyle lived out in an ever-shrinking geography. She worked out in her house and jogged only on the streets of her gated community. She refused even to go to the grocery store, despite the inconvenience to her husband.

In this minimal world she exercised perfect control. Her life shrank as her world shrank. Things had to be in the same place at all times. Routines became religious rituals. She insisted on perfect control over a perfectly tiny world.

Counselor: Were you afraid of your mother?

Susan: Only when she was drunk.

Counselor: Which was often.

Susan: Very often.

Counselor: So you were very afraid, very often.

Susan: I think I was always afraid.

Counselor: Is fear your most common childhood memory?

Susan: Yes. I was always afraid.

Counselor: Would you characterize your home as chaotic?

Susan: It was a zoo.

Counselor: A fearful little girl all alone in an uncontrolled environment, right?

Susan: Right.

Counselor: You longed for order.

Susan: Yes.

Counselor: Any order in your world was created by you?

Susan: Sometimes my room was the only neat place in our house.

Counselor: Sometimes?

Susan: OK, most of the time.

Counselor: Your life felt, what, out of control?

Susan: Yes. Totally out of control. Everything was out of control. My parents were always screaming at each other. My mother was a binge drinker. My life was a nightmare.

When she began this speech, she was weeping. When she finished it, she was sobbing. The onion skins peeled back layer by layer, the tears increasing at each layer. At the end was her longing for an ordered world, and at the core of that was her inability to trust anyone else to provide it.

Unless a child learns to trust, her world of chaos is threatening and unnerving. She longs for trust and all that it means: calmness, security, confidence, well-being. She battles for inner calm. It will not come. Someone else has controlled her entire life. More precisely her world is utterly out of control because of someone else's life. She wants a loving, trusting relationship, but she cannot get there. Anything that threatens her fortress life is her enemy. She tightens the controls—tighter and tighter until all love, affection, relationships, and joy are squeezed out. The less there is in her life, the less there is to disrupt it. She is in control, utterly, because she is the only one to be trusted.

Having broken through the trust barrier, Susan could now begin the therapy of trust. The counselor began with the most basic trust question: Is there anything, absolutely anything, for which she could trust God? In high school Susan had "prayed the sinner's prayer" at a youth camp and learned that she should trust God for eternal life.

Counselor: Do you? Do you trust Him for eternal life?

Susan: I think so. Yes, I do.

Counselor: So if you were to die today, you believe you would go to heaven.

Susan: Yes.

Counselor: To what extent?

Susan: I don't understand the question.

Counselor: On a scale of one to ten how much do you believe this?

Susan: I don't know how to put a number to it.

Counselor: Try.

Susan: Do you realize how irritating you can be?

Counselor: I've been told. Now try.

Susan: OK. Eight. No, nine. Nine.

Counselor: Why not ten? I'm just wondering.

Susan: I don't really know. It just seems as though you should say nine.

Counselor: Instead of ten?

Susan: Yes.

Counselor: In other words, on a doubt scale of one to ten, you doubt God at one.

Susan: What?

Counselor: If you trust Him at nine, you must doubt Him at one.

Susan: I never thought of it like that. No, I do not doubt God. Not even at one.

Counselor: Then again, one to ten, how much do you trust God for eternal life?

Susan: Ten. Definitely ten. If I were to die right now, I know I would go to heaven.

Counselor: Based on His Word?

Susan: Yes, the Bible. I know the blood of Jesus saves.

Counselor: Not on your works?

Susan: No. I know better than that.

Counselor: You cannot arrange or provide for your own salvation.

Susan: No.

Counselor: That is trust. Do you trust God for that?

Susan: Yes, I trust Him for that.

Counselor: Then we start there.

Over the months ahead, two steps forward and one back, Susan and the counselor built on that single building block, an edifice of trust. What else could she trust God for? Forgiveness. What else? The trust mechanism destroyed by her home life was gradually rebuilt. Promise by promise. Verse by verse. It was a long journey, but trust built trust. It was like accrued interest. The better she got at trusting God, the better she got.

She could trust Him for breakfast. Give us this day our daily bread. Lunch, the same. Dinner, the same. She could trust Him for her body, trust Him for safety, trust Him for total authority over her life. Total trust means yielding total control. Total control.

Counselor: Close your eyes and imagine what I tell you.

Susan: I have never been very good at imagining things.

Counselor: Try. I want you to see yourself as a small child. Can you do that?

Susan: Yes.

Counselor: Now, is there a voice of one behind you? It is your heavenly Father. Keep your eyes closed and listen. "I am the God who ordered the universe, and I can be trusted. Do you trust?"

Susan: Am I supposed to answer that?

Counselor: Do you have an answer?

Susan: Yes, I do.

Counselor: Then answer Him. Not me. Him.

Susan: *Hesitantly,* Yes, Lord, I do trust You.

Counselor: Utterly?

Susan: Utterly.

Counselor: Then fall back in My arms, and let Me catch you.

Susan: What? Eyes wide open?

Counselor: It's a child's game. Most fathers play it at some time or another.

Susan: It's stupid.

Counselor: Is it?

Susan: Well, I didn't play it.

Counselor: We're talking about a different Father here.

Susan: I don't believe in a God who plays games.

Counselor: Try, just for a moment.

Susan: *Eyes closed again.* This is stupid.

Counselor: Indulge me. Now see that little girl. See, her eyes are shut tight. Do you see her?

Susan: Yes.

Counselor: Her heavenly Father is behind. His arms are outstretched to catch her. Can you visualize that?

Susan: Not so well.

Counselor: Fall back. He says keep your eyes closed and fall back into My arms. I promise I'll catch you.

Susan: She can't do it.

Counselor: Order her to. Call her by name and command her to do it.

Susan: I can't. Not today. *Eyes open again.*

Counselor: That's OK.

Susan: Is it? Can we stop now?

Counselor: Of course.

Susan: I'm sorry to disappoint you.

Counselor: You didn't. I was so proud of you.

Susan: You were? Why?

Counselor: You got very close. Very close to the next step is a good one, a big one, and you got very close. I was so proud of you.

Susan: Maybe next time I can do it.

Counselor: Maybe. We'll see. Soon anyway, I can tell.

Susan: I'm going to eat with my husband tonight at a restaurant.

Counselor: Bon appétit.

Susan: Very funny.

Susan's story was full of setbacks, as so many are, but the key to her wholeness was trust. Simple platitudes like "let go and let God" filled Susan with terror. She could not let go, and she could not let God. She had to be in control. To begin her healing, she had to come to grips with a potentially life-threatening condition. That therapeutic trek to trust was painful enough. Calling it what it was—anorexia—was no less excruciating for Susan than for alcoholics or addicts. All those we've met in these pages had to come to this point. Johnny had to call *rape* what it was. The word *pimp* was horrible and horribly necessary for Edith. And for Susan there was no way except through the word *anorexia*.

Having to reach that plateau, however, she had to trudge on to trust. It was brutal therapy indeed. Susan had to pry loose her definition of God from her chaotic experiences with her parents. Using biblical promises, memorizing and repeating them thousands of times, Susan began to reimage a God who could be trusted, who must be trusted in fact for wholeness.

JOHNNY'S PROCESS

An acidic cynicism shadowed Johnny's relationships—in fact it covered his entire worldview. His dark humor drifted toward bitterness. Nothing was as it seemed. Nothing would turn out right. His jokes became harsher, his put-downs became meaner, and his side comments, loaded with a sneer, took on a sharpness that cut into the joy of all those around him.

As Johnny and the counselor worked backward toward the attack that had left him so wounded, they encountered a wall along the way. Johnny's fear of that wall was the haunting terror that others, particularly his wife, would come to know what only Johnny and the counselor now know.

Johnny: Do I have to tell her?

Counselor: Don't you think she has a right to know?

Johnny: Why should she?

Counselor: You are one. You and your wife are one heart and one flesh. What happened to you is between you. When she knows it, it's gone, a wall demolished.

Johnny: Why should she have that picture in her mind?

Counselor: Don't you think she can handle it?

Johnny: What will she think of me?

Counselor: What does she think of you now? You've already just about destroyed any love she ever had for you. You did that by keeping her out. It makes you wonder what might happen if you let her in.

Johnny: I just can't stand the thought of it.

Counselor: Who is it you don't trust, her or you?

Johnny: Have you ever been told that you talk mostly in questions?

Counselor: Yes, I have.

Johnny: And do you know that it is a very irritating habit?

Counselor: Is it?

Johnny: Oh, that's *good*. That's really good.

Johnny has spent more than forty years not trusting anyone with what happened to him. He did not trust his parents or his wife. He did not trust himself. He did not look at it or call it what it was. He shut it away from the light of day, never even trusting his own mind to bear the memory. And God? Never. Not even once in those forty years did he even pray about it.

Johnny had to make a leap into the dark, right out into outer space. He had to tell out loud what had never been told, what had not in fact been consciously thought. It was like plunging over a precipice. Was it that she would despise him? As the counselor said, she could hardly think less of him. Was he really concerned that she could not handle it? He had faced the fact years earlier that she was tougher than he was. It was none of these things.

Hiding had become a mental habit for Johnny. *Don't let anyone in very far.* Even long after he was no longer conscious of what he was hiding, hiding was simply easier, at least less frightening, than disclosure. Keep everyone back, even his wife, at a distance, behind a wall. It was not lying. It was separation. Yes, that's what it was, he told himself; a proper distance is the key to proper respect. Maintain some privacy. Keep the door locked. Walls make good neighbors, and good neighbors should stay behind the walls. Wives also. Keep your wife at arm's length. Let her in, but only so far. What are you hiding?

JENNY'S JOURNEY

Jenny, for her part, was raised in an emotional desert. Her parents were not so much harsh and unreasonable as they were utterly detached. Her longing for parental encouragement drove her to be an overachiever, often in extracurricular activities at which she was not naturally gifted. Girls' basketball was the perfect example. She played her heart out, but she was hardly a star. She became her team's hardest-working team player; the girl won the admiration of her coaches and teammates. She did not, however, win anything from her parents, who never attended a single game, nor from her brothers, who scorned her efforts and mocked her every achievement, not just in sports but in academics, school politics, and her church youth group.

She confided in the counselor that among her most painful memories was reading a children's book in which the mother would comb her little girl's hair and sing to her as she did. She said she could not imagine her mother singing to her under any circumstances. She teared up even in telling about the book. She longed to be held and kissed and sung to. She ached to be cherished in the bosom of the kind of loving family she saw only in books.

Counselor: She never sang to you? Not ever?

Jenny: Never. We just didn't do that kind of thing in my house.

Counselor: Surely you were hugged occasionally. Weren't you at least hugged good night? Surely sometimes.

Jenny: Never. Not once that I can remember. Not once.

Hugging and affection did not come easily to Jenny. Indeed, it was hard emotional work. The same fears of affection hampered her sex life in the early years of her marriage. Lingering kisses made her apprehensive. Her fear of intimacy made her less than enthusiastic about the entire process of sex.

Her childhood was one long rejection. The scars on her inner child were not put there by trauma, but they were there

COURAGE TO BE HEALED

nonetheless. She wanted what she had never known and feared what she wanted: intimacy. The rejected child within her ached for acceptance and feared intimacy. Conflicted and fearful, Jenny found in her relationship with Christ the acceptance she ached for, but her inner wounds made it easy for her to see the failings of others as rejection of her. *Nothing in particular. That's just the way I am. I have never been very good at—well—intimacy.*

As I mentioned, Johnny did eventually tell his wife what had happened to him. She handled it well, lovingly in fact, and with sensitive understanding, but he felt as though his skin were being peeled off. The lonely pain of living behind a shield Johnny discerned as nothing compared with the agony of self-revelation. Cold separation, emotional distance had become a manageable defense mechanism for Johnny, indeed a way of life. It turned out to be infinitely more expensive than he imagined it could be. Truth and trust were as gut-wrenching as he had feared. They turned out to be infinitely more beneficial than he ever could have imagined.

The ultimate crisis that blew Johnny and Jenny's marriage open and finally forced Johnny to seek the healing he needed also blew Jenny's world apart. It was not entirely a surprise. It was the years leading up to the explosion. Johnny's level of toxic misery had begun to spill out onto her. His distance became worse every day. Every attempt to reach him was met with a brick wall. Her fear and loneliness had built up to a breaking point, so the final break was not a surprise. Even so, she was shocked, disappointed, betrayed, furious, and afraid. This had the potential to destroy her world. What about her children? What about her home? What about the entire world as she knew it?

When Johnny started therapy, she was skeptical, to say the least. Nothing in his life had led her to believe he would follow through. Would he bail out on the process, her, or any future they might have? She thought he would. Then where would she be?

Every negative emotion rioted inside her, and to make matters worse, she felt robbed of her support lines. The professionals seemed to have a single focus—Johnny. Get Johnny through; counsel Johnny; help Johnny; heal Johnny; don't let Johnny do something desperate. Johnny was depressed. Johnny was humiliated. Of course he was. But what about Jenny?

With some professional help and the grace of God, Jenny began to hack her way through the jungle of hurt to a base camp of forgiveness, then to understanding, and finally to health. She began to discover her own childhood hurt: rejection.

Counselor: Tell me the most painful memory of your childhood.

Jenny: My mother was about to take my oldest brother somewhere in the car. I don't even remember where. As they started out to the car, I heard my mother laugh. It was a warm and casual laugh. It seemed as if she and my brother were laughing at some secret. It was so out of the ordinary to hear her laugh like that; I was shocked.

I yelled out to her, "What are you laughing about?"

She didn't even look back at me. She just yelled, "It doesn't concern you!"

I called, "Please let me come with you!"

Again, she didn't even look at me. She just yelled, "Go back in the house!"

That seemed like my whole family experience. No intimacy. No love. No laughter. Or at least what there was wasn't for me. I just stood there crying. Rejected.

Counselor: That didn't feel good, did it?

Jenny: No, it didn't, and it just about sums up my entire childhood. Now Johnny has rejected me. My whole life—one huge rejection.

Counselor: Don't you think your parents loved you?

Jenny: Maybe. How would you know if somebody loves you if they don't tell you? All my effort at sports and good grades. Nothing. Nobody ever said, "We love you, and we are proud of you."

Counselor: Never?

Jenny: Never. Neither my mother nor my father ever said the words. Ever. I was never hugged, never tucked in at night, never affirmed. I never heard, "We are proud of you." All the things I did in school—cheerleading, school offices, my grades—I never once heard, "We love you, and we're proud of you." And now Johnny's done this to me. This is my whole life.

It was the perfect storm. A performance-oriented, driven workaholic married to a woman still hurting from a childhood of emotional deprivation, if not abuse. Both deeply wounded, one by trauma and the other by the slow pain of a cold and loveless childhood.

Jenny's suffering was intense and intensely lonely. In an effort to minimize the public explosion of the marital crisis, especially the collateral damage to their children, Johnny and Jenny decided to seek help as privately as possible. Near a breakdown and riddled with guilt and emotional anguish, Johnny immediately became the object of the healing effort.

Jenny suffered in silence. This only served to magnify her sense of loneliness and rejection. Her private pain was made worse by watching all the efforts being poured out on Johnny.

Jenny did most of her work directly with the Wonderful Counselor. His love, His acceptance, was the healing grace she needed. As she began to move further and further into divine acceptance and to become ever more aware of the Father's love, her family's rejection lost most of its destructive power. Likewise, Johnny's failure began to lose its ability to energize all that childhood pain. Jenny entered into a place of healing with the Wonderful Counselor, a deep place that few ever access, especially without a lot of professional help. It was not easy for her to get there. She limped her way into the holy place. She found there the warm embrace, the full acceptance, of her Father.

The slow trauma of rejection is poison to the soul. Every incident that feels remotely like rejection adds to that toxic flow. It colors one's worldview in somber shades of gray. One person's act or acts of rejection become everyone's. All have rejected. No one loves me. No one really wants me.

The next step is the deadly one. *There must be something wrong with me. If everyone rejects me, then it must be because I merit rejection. There must be something, some hidden, mysterious thing, that not even I can see that keeps me from being fully accepted and truly loved.*

Jenny, by the grace of the Wonderful Counselor, worked her way back from that far country, but it was a long, torturous trek. Johnny was raped. Jenny was rejected. Johnny wanted admiration, longed for it, ached to believe that others could not see and would never know that nasty thing that made him unacceptable. Jenny wanted intimacy. She just wanted that laughing family to open the door and welcome her in from the hallway. She was intimacy deprived, and she wanted intimacy from a man who was terrified of intimacy. He wanted intimacy but had few clues what it even looked like. Their collision was a nightmare of broken dreams.

Their therapy of trust was a mutually agreed-upon torture. Johnny had to trust his hidden secret to her. She had to release her fear of rejection and learn again to trust the very man who had bitterly rejected her. The therapy was painful. It always is. The therapy of trust was terrifying. We can pour the toxin of rejection into others without even realizing it.

At one megachurch I pastored, there was a Christian school. A certain girl was accused by her classmates of some minor misbehavior. As I remember it, the whole matter was over hardly anything at all. Her "punishment," such as it was, involved writing a one-page paper explaining why sixth-grade girls shouldn't throw spit wads or whatever. The whole thing went sideways because of three things. The teacher and half the class saw her do it, whatever it was. She denied it. And her father became the avenging angel.

Of course it all finally wound up in my office. The teacher looked mortified, the little girl looked terrified, and the father looked as if he was ready to go to war with the Marines to defend his daughter's innocence. After a few moments it became obvious that the girl had done it, had denied it in a weak moment, and now couldn't back down. Her father was the reason for that.

"Look, sir," I said, "you do realize, don't you, that she did it. This teacher and all these students are not in some mass conspiracy."

He was stunned at this outrageous comment. "I realize no such thing!" he shouted. "She told me she didn't do it."

"Look," I said, "she's not the first little girl to get caught up in some silly little lie to keep from getting in trouble."

"My daughter would never lie to me," he announced.

The look on that child's face still haunts me. I could see in her eyes what that meant to her. If she ever did lie to him, she knew she would no longer be his daughter. That is rejection.

I suppose the last word on whether inner healing "works" in a life cannot be written until that life is over. If the counselor and the client claim victory too soon, lapsing or backsliding is always possible. On the other hand, we need not wait for the casket to be lowered and the epitaph carved before a good report can be given.

Johnny and Jenny are the poster couple for this book, the clients who dealt with more wounds, showed more courage, and believed God for more healing than anyone could have imagined at the beginning. Their report is not the rote praise report from testimony time at the Wednesday night service. Their report is a beautiful one filled with grace and peace and healing at the end of a long and painful journey. Both Johnny and Jenny had to hack through their own dark jungles, and neither could really help the other. Each was looking for healing, yet when they came to a clearing in the jungle, they found not just their Healer but each other. Their relationship, and they state this categorically, is better than ever, better than it was even in the first years of their marriage.

They testify to victory, and they give God the glory. That has to be enough for the rest of us.

So much of the search for inner healing is exactly that, a search. And a search is a process. Americans, maybe everyone, want the finish line rather than the race. Yet the race must be run. On the other hand, it's wrong to make inner healing sound like a race without the victor's crown. There is victory. Real victory. And it is sweet indeed.

I spent a year counseling with a young attorney on the verge of a nervous breakdown. The whole year, every time we talked, all we talked about was that God is "nice." Just that. This man was a driven professional serving a driving God. When he became convinced, truly convinced in the core of his being, that God is *nice*, healing flooded his life. His also is a testimony of victory. Peace. Rest. A nice God. And victory.

All this is to say stay in the process. Don't bail out. Keep hacking away at the jungle. But remember, the journey is not the point. Victory is the point, and victory is ahead.

Chapter 5

—◆◆◆—

PETER: A BIBLICAL PICTURE
OF BROKENNESS HEALED

A S Monty Python often said, "Now for something completely different."

This chapter will be like nothing else in the book. One minister's objection to counseling was that Jesus never did it. Certainly that is correct in the sense that Jesus did not keep office hours or meet with scheduled clients in his office. On the other hand, neither did He attend board meetings, and I assure you that pastor went to plenty of those. Jesus' "counseling sessions" were spontaneous and contextual, but they quite frequently bore the earmarks of biblical counseling.

Jesus did grief counseling with the disciples on the road to

Emmaus. In John chapter 3 He met in the dark of the night with a client named Nicodemus, who was struggling with a religious spirit, was filled with biblical confusion, and had deep insecurities about eternal life. In John chapter 4 Jesus did counseling with a guilt-ridden woman with a sordid past and a heart riddled with racial hurt.

In John 21 Jesus' lakeside encounter with a hurting man affords a touching and powerful insight into Christ as the Wonderful Counselor. Here then is a view of a counseling session, if you will. Jesus is the counselor. The client's name is Simon Peter, a commercial fisherman. His wounded emotions raw from a recent and very public failure, this businessman is like almost every counseling client I've ever encountered. He deeply wants and desperately needs soul restoration, but he fears the very meeting where that is most likely to happen.

The hope so recently drained out of him, drained as utterly as death, was just beginning to struggle back to life. Only just beginning, though, and with strength as faint as a whisper. Despair and guilt—most of all guilt—lay upon that hope like a massive stone. Until that stone was rolled away—well, what was the use of even thinking like that? His remorse was unrelenting and as useless as it was permanent.

Now, this confusion, these strange occurrences, stirred the faint whisper of hope like a breeze. But to what avail? What should he believe? He had grown up believing his eyes. Now his eyes told contradicting stories. Should he believe what he had seen for three glorious years? Or what he had seen over the space of a few horrific hours? Or should he believe the bizarre, dreamlike visions of the last few days? Maybe that's what they were: visions milky and confusing like sleepwalking then waking to remember only distorted images in the half-light. Which was more real, the sleepwalking of hope or the raw awakened pain of condemnation?

He could bear it no longer. He was not a mystical or contemplative man. He was a man of action. Real things, real work, real sweat, that's what he needed now. He needed the sun blazing on his naked back as it bent to a familiar task. This weepy, mysterious cloud of unknowing seemed somehow womanly. He needed to flee into a rough and manly reality, to strain at the labor of his youth. He could not silence his aching guilt and dared not indulge himself in feathery hope. His desiccated soul needed solace. The company of men. Their laughter. Man's work. That's what he needed, and he knew exactly where to find it.

"I am going fishing."

They stared at him for a moment but quickly, as though they had been thinking this very thought. Then they chimed in. "We are coming with you. Yes, that's what we all need to do. To the lake. To work. Enough of this dream life."

"So that's it then," someone asked, "we're going back to fishing?"

"What do you mean back?" he snapped. "What do you mean by that? I said I'm going fishing, not back to fishing."

After that no one said much of anything for a long while. In fact hardly anyone spoke all night. He had always enjoyed a long night's fishing. The cool breeze, men's jokes and men's laughter, the jovial unity of men in a boat. Then the morning sun, the new heat on his shoulders, the dawn dancing on the water's surface. These things he knew. These things were real. The "back to fishing" remark still rankled, but he was in a boat doing what he knew, what he loved, real work for a man's body if not for his very soul. He was a big man, and he needed to work.

This night was a disappointment, however, as was the fishing. It seemed to him a picture of what had become of his life. The boisterous brotherhood he had hoped for had been spoiled by his sour thoughts. He felt disconnected from the others, and he thought perhaps their own silence was unspoken condemnation. Every man in the boat knew what he had done, and the shameful knowledge lay heavy upon the little boat in thick and uncomfortable silence.

The fact that they worked all night in utter futility only added to his heaviness. Time after time they drew in the empty nets. Was fishing also ruined for him? More precisely, had he ruined it? Even this? Even fishing? A failure, guilt ridden, empty-handed, and humiliated, he finished mechanically, joylessly, knowing that these nets would be empty even before they were brought up.

THE DAWNING

As the morning sun gained power, he shucked off his coat to bake his aching muscles. They all looked at him and stretched as if to say, "That's it. Haul them in, and let's go home." They bent to the final task without a word. They had all done this before, a thousand times, though seldom with such utter failure, such heaviness.

"Have you caught anything?"

The shouted question was from a stranger on the shore. It was the kind of good-natured question all fishermen have asked each other through the ages, but this morning it stung more than it should have.

"No," someone in the back yelled as they piled their nets in the bottom of the boat and started to set the oars. "No luck tonight."

"Cast on the right side. There. Yes, right there. You'll catch them there."

The morning sun was behind the man, and the brilliant glare off the water was blinding. Shielding their eyes, they peered across the lake at the stranger but could not make him out. Then, oddly, without even discussing it, they did exactly as he said. As they had done countless times in their lives and as they had done all that night with nothing to show for it, they cast a net. After watching its weighted perimeter spread the net in a wide circle, then splash softly and sink, they waited for it to settle before drawing the draglines. As soon as they did, they knew it was full. Their experienced muscles told them that this single cast was a long night's harvest. Expressions of surprise and shared laughter began to fill the boat even before the bulging nets surfaced. Their spirits lifted. This was more like it. When they could finally see the thrashing silvery bodies of what appeared to be more fish than they had ever taken in a single cast, they began to speak as workers do, to advise each other.

"Easy over there on that side."

"Not too fast! Not so fast."

"Get them on in. The nets will break."

In the midst of it John let go of his hold and stood upright in the boat. Shielding his eyes one more time, he peered again at the man on the shore. John's lips moved, but at first he said nothing aloud. Then not as much to them as to himself, he whispered.

"It's the Lord."

This statement hit the big man like a fist to his jaw. "Wha...?"

"I tell you, it's Him, Peter. That's the Lord over there."

The others paused, holding the nets, waiting to see for themselves but loathing to lose their marvelous catch. Like John, Peter simply loosed his hold and stood. Seizing his cloak, he shrugged it on over his head and plunged into the lake. The others were not entirely surprised. This was Peter all over. He always plunged into things, into everything. Let him go on ahead. They wanted these fish, and if they all did as Peter had done, who would bring in the boat? Even John put his hands back to the task. Let Peter go on ahead. Maybe...well, that was Peter's business.

Peter dragged himself up out of the lake and onto the black stones of the shoreline. His bare feet struggled to find balance on the rocks, and his clothes hung as heavy and sodden as his soul.

Oh God, how he dreaded this.

Dreaded it like a beating.

And yet somehow he longed for it, ached for it. That's why he left the others in the boat and swam ashore in the chilly dawn. If this man was Jesus, and now Peter was certain He was, the coming rebuke would be as crushing as it was deserved. Perhaps even final. Maybe Peter would be banished, sent away in disgrace.

Well, let it happen in private. If Jesus intended to give him a tongue-lashing or cast him away, Peter wanted to hear it alone. On the other hand, there was always the chance for grace. Peter had seen Jesus forgive and heal some of the nastiest people in the world. Perhaps—but there was no use speculating. Jesus was there. Right there in front of him. Sitting by a fire.

Shivering now, Peter crept closer. A smile played across Jesus' face. Peter instinctively stretched his hands toward the charcoal fire and lifted his face to meet the gaze of Jesus.

A memory, not one from long in the past but a recent and new memory, instantly vaulted into his mind. Peter saw himself standing in Caiaphas' courtyard, shivering on that fearful night just as he did now. He heard his own voice. *I never heard of this Jesus. Never heard of Him, I tell you.* He saw it all, heard it all, and it seemed that somehow past and present became one. There also had been a charcoal fire. There also he had warmed himself. The door of Caiaphas' house opened, and they led Jesus out in bonds. Peter's eyes met the eyes of Jesus across the fire. Which fire? Some rooster somewhere announced the approach of dawn. Startled, Peter jumped at the sound, uncertain if it was real or the tortured voice of his memories.

Their eyes met. Neither man spoke.

The horrible memory hung in the air between them.

"Come and Dine"

Then Jesus spread His hands as if to indicate the fish grilling over the coals and the bread baking on the hot flat stones at the fire's edges.

Peter glanced at the food being cooked, then back at Jesus. What did it mean? What did Jesus want? Should Peter speak? All Peter's practiced confessions stuck in his throat. At last it was Jesus who broke the silence. He smiled.

"Come and dine."

There are only two places in the New Testament in which a reference is made to a "charcoal fire." One is the story we are immersed in here. The other is the fire in Caiaphas' courtyard. The very fire that night at which Peter warmed his hands is described as a charcoal fire. Two charcoal fires in all the New Testament: one in the story of Peter's betrayal; one now, in this story, as Jesus gazes at His betrayer.

Yet it was not to hurt Peter's heart that Jesus met him by a charcoal fire. It was to heal and restore Peter. There is no biblical record of a stern rebuke. No tongue-lashing. No demand that Peter make some humiliating public confession of the kind so beloved by the modern church. Just breakfast. Bread and fish and fellowship.

"Come and dine."

In a certain survey I heard about, Americans were asked what they most longed to hear someone say to them. Of all the answers given, three were the most common. The first was entirely predictable: "I love you." Americans, no less I suppose than anyone else in the world, want to know they are loved and relish hearing it said to them. The second most common answer surprised me: "I forgive you." We are guilty, and we know we are. Our ache for absolution makes this simple phrase our hearts' cry. Forgiveness, human and divine, is a deep need, but I was surprised that it was expressed so commonly.

The third answer really gave me a laugh: "Supper's ready." That was a surprise to me. The third answer seems so frivolous compared with our felt need for love and forgiveness.

Then it hit me. That is the whole gospel. That is what Jesus was saying to Peter on the shore of the lake of Tiberius. That is in fact the threefold announcement at every communion service. Every time the church is invited to the Lord's table, every time the elements are offered, the message from God is always the same:

"I love you."

"I forgive you."

"Supper's ready."

Preemptory grace disallowed Peter's confession, made unnecessary any penitence before full immediate restoration. If our every sin is a denial of Christ, then Peter was every one of us at our worst.

Peter denied Christ three times. Perhaps, probably in fact, Peter repented and determined within himself to do better each time. *I wasn't prepared. Just let them ask me again. Just let that particular temptation come again. This time I am ready. This time I won't fail.*

But fail he did. Again, and yet again.

The question is not so much about where Jesus was at that moment on the beach. He was full of the grace that He offered Peter—along with breakfast. We know where Jesus was because of what He did and what He said and did not say. We also know because we know where Jesus already is. His grace is majestic.

The question is, Where was Peter? What condition was he in that morning? I believe he was in a hard place, a very lonely and pain-filled place. I believe this was because Peter was a man, a human being who had failed horribly and publicly, and human nature has not changed from that time to this.

Peter had known ministry and worked miracles. He had cast out demons and healed the sick. Beyond all that, he had walked with Jesus, seen the transfiguration, and heard the audible voice of God. And yet he fell. He failed the greatest test of his life to that point, and all his colleagues knew it. A fallen minister, shivering, guilty, and longing for help. Where was he that morning?

He was at the very doorway of wholeness. That doorway is called brokenness. Peter was broken. But now he could be whole.

The twenty-first chapter of John, which contains the narrative you've just read, is a beautiful story. It is an encouraging one, to say the least. But is it really a look at wonderful counsel?

Beside the Sea of Galilee today, perched on the jagged rocks at its pebbled shoreline, is a small chapel called The Church of the Primacy of Saint Peter. It is a beautiful spot and one of my favorites in all of Israel. I love to go there. There is only one problem: the place is misnamed. It should be called The Church of the Restoration of Saint Peter, or The Church of Soul Restoration, or The Church of Inner Healing, or perhaps The Church of Wonderful Counsel, because that is what happened there.

THE PROCESS OF HEALING

There, or somewhere near there, Peter met Jesus in that dawn reunion, and the two of them joined the others in a simple breakfast of fish and bread. At that moment of renewed fellowship Peter's guilt-ridden and shame-filled soul was healed. He was also, of course, reaffirmed in ministry and leadership, but first, and most importantly, Peter was healed.

Three important characteristics of that lakeside encounter clearly make it a lovely example of the process of inner healing. First, Jesus took Peter back to the painful point of his personal failure. At the moment Peter stretched his hands out across that charcoal fire, and his eyes met the eyes of Jesus; his pathetic denial confronted him like a slap in the face.

No one wants to see his own failures for what they are. No one enjoys being confronted by his darkest depravity. No one wants to revisit the scene of a dreadful horror, of some violent and traumatic incident. Absolutely no one wants to be taken there again, forced to see it, even reenter it, and feel its pain all over again. Yet in order for Peter to receive the dawn of a new day of healing and renewal, Jesus re-created the midnight scene of Peter's dark denial.

Just as Johnny had to dredge up the deeply buried scene of his humiliation, Jesus surprised Peter with the dramatic re-creation of Peter's courtyard denial only days before.

Not only did Jesus take Peter back there; He met Peter there—went into the scene with Peter and comforted him there. Wonderful counsel disallows denial. The wounded cannot be made whole without facing the wound, the "awful moment," whatever it is. Just seeing it, just "going there," is not enough and could in fact be devastating. They must encounter Jesus there, right there, right in the midst of the "awful moment."

When Peter saw that charcoal fire, when he extended his hands for warmth, just as he had in Caiaphas' courtyard, his eyes met Jesus' eyes. Jesus was there, in it, in the scene, in the "awful moment," and in His eyes Peter saw love and healing grace. This grace is at the very heart of soul restoration. The "awful moment" must be reentered, but not alone, not without Jesus. The midnight moment revisited must give way to the dawn of Jesus' healing presence. In Jesus' presence the two moments merge into one, and both are healed.

It was not to humiliate Peter that the betrayal was

re-created in such detail. It was to say to Peter, "I was there. I still loved you there. Now I'm here, and I still love you."

Jesus did not stop there. Hardly. He took Peter deeper into the bitter scene. Notice the re-created repetition. Peter denied Jesus three times, and three times Jesus asked the question "Do you love Me?"

What was Jesus after? Peter's humiliation? Certainly not. Three times Peter had publicly denied even knowing Jesus. Such a sin could only be healed by visiting "the scene of the crime." Peter had to see what he had done for what it was, but having seen, he needed to know that Jesus, who had also seen it, still loved him. Beyond that Jesus wanted to restore Peter's love.

Three times Peter answered the questions in the courtyard with denial. That is why Jesus asked him three times, "Do you love Me?" It was not to hurt Peter but to remind him that despite a momentary failure, Peter truly loved the Lord. Jesus knew Peter loved Him. He knew He needed to remind Peter.

It is worth noting that having restored the relationship, Jesus then restored Peter's calling to ministry and leadership. Here then is the pattern of soul restoration. Jesus' pattern is remarkably different from many in ecclesiastical circles. They seem to relish exposure, humiliation, and public rejection for private sin. In the face of very public sin, Jesus chose private healing, private restoration, and a renewed call to ministry. Here is Jesus' pattern: When sin and denial lead to guilt and separation, prevenient grace forces us to see, to really revisit what we have done and recognize it for what it was. For healing from inflicted trauma He does the same. He takes us back there, back into it all to see it for what it really was. Then Jesus enters that scene and reassures us of His love. Then He reminds us of our love for Him. Finally He reassures us that we are not disqualified. Soul restoration cannot be complete without the restoration of fellowship.

As their eyes met across the glowing coals, Peter knew that Jesus knew about the three denials. The terrible pain of the moment must have pierced Peter like a sword. But only for a moment. Jesus' eyes were not filled with hurt and recrimination. His were eyes of compassion and restoration.

So far so good, but one more step had to be completed. Peter had to be brought back into full relationship. Broken fellowship had to be restored. That could only happen in divine communion, in the breaking of bread. It was to a *meal* that Jesus summoned Peter and the others, as He had done at just such crucial moments throughout their few brief years together.

There is no way to understand that moment on the lakeshore apart from brokenness. Peter could never have swum to shore, would never have braved the encounter, unless he was a broken man.

Brokenness changed Peter not for the worse but for a new kind of ministry and for eternity. Peter's total brokenness was necessary for him to realize his need for total healing, but Peter could not heal himself. Peter could not restore himself to relationship with Christ or to his destiny in the church. Only Jesus could do that, and He did it as He does even now at the table of grace.

The New Testament writings of Peter reveal in a spectacular way the amazing transformation wrought in his life. They also tell us that we too can be transformed through brokenness.

The beauty of language, the ability of a mind inspired to put into words elevated, enabling thoughts, is a gift to humanity. To say things, great, mysterious things, and to say them eloquently has often been the reserve of the brilliant and well educated. Shakespeare, Wordsworth, Dumas, and King David. The haunting soliloquies of Hamlet and the sweet unalloyed tones of Psalm 23—these words touch the soul in some secret place.

Now pause your reading here, and open your Bible and read 1 Peter 2:5–10. Read those words, and meditate not so much on their content (not that that isn't the most important part of it) but on the sensitive, intelligent beauty of expression. Allow yourself to be impressed with the word selection, the cadence, the inside and simplicity of the structure. The language. Just look at the language. Surely these are the words of a true poet, not just of some overeducated genius possessed of a high IQ but unable to express himself. These were surely penned by a great mind, a great spirit who thought deeply, who looked within and learned, perhaps by years of literary training, to write what he beheld in such beauty that readers, even the ones who despise the theology, would be forced to relish the sheer wonder of the language.

Now read this sentence: "a light that shines in a dark place, until the day dawns and the morning star rises in your hearts" (2 Pet. 1:19).

Beautiful.

Or this: "an inheritance incorruptible and undefiled and that does not fade away" (1 Pet. 1:4).

Even the atheist, hardened in his hatred for God, can surely appreciate this language for its own sake and must surely read this with appreciation for its lyrical timing.

Even if one doubted the truth of the words, disbelieved the

inheritance and hated the theology, the words are undeniably perfect. They are golden apples in a silver bowl and surely the work of a seasoned literary genius who has honed his skills to perfection.

Not so. They are among the few preserved writings of a blue-collar, working-class man of whose education we know nothing beyond what we may assume based on his Jewish culture. "He was ignorant and unlearned," we are told.

This was the same man who, during the horrible night of Christ's arrest and bogus trial, denied any knowledge of Jesus of Nazareth. Not only did Peter deny Jesus; he denied Him three times, having been warned in advance that he would. It was not as though he was taken by surprise. From a dark night of devastating personal moral failure to a place of primal apostolic leadership and truly insightful eloquence, a new and powerful voice arose from the ashes of shame. But how? What happened?

Pentecost, certainly. The experience of the Upper Room was the empowering moment. The cowardice of Caiaphas' house gone, Peter roared like the Lion of Judah in his Pentecostal message of Acts 2. What boldness! Pentecostal power, to be sure. But what got him to the Upper Room? Why was he even allowed to be there at all? Judas Iscariot was not there. His unavailing remorse found suicidal expression. Peter was also remorseful. What was the difference? There was very little difference in what they had done. Judas denied Jesus for money. Peter denied Him out of cowardice. Judas denied Jesus once. Peter denied Him three times after being told that he would. Both were sorry. Judas tried to give the money back. Peter wept. Both sinned; both failed; both were remorseful. One hanged himself, and the other became a saint.

The standard, and correct, answer of course is Peter's Pentecostal experience. But there is more, and we often miss it. What happened to Peter between Caiaphas' house and the Upper Room that did not happen to Judas? Before Pentecost. What? Something, but what?

A fishing trip and a single word: brokenness.

Chapter 6

―――✦◆✦―――

THE TOXIN
OF CONDEMNATION

TOXIN	THRONE	THERAPY	GOAL
Condemnation	Idolatry	Worship	Balance

MARTHA WAS AN eighteen-year-old college freshman who was completely convinced she was unattractive. Her decision to attend a state university three states away from her family had left her friendless and alone. That she was attending a secular school made matters worse. It also didn't help that her roommate at that school was Martha's opposite in nearly every way. The girl was vivacious, attractive, slim, and exceptionally worldly. She was also an experienced bisexual. Martha was easy pickings.

Martha's suicide attempt before the Thanksgiving break

of her first semester in college stunned her parents. She was sent home, of course. Her parents were terrified and in shock. In counseling Martha stonewalled for weeks. She deflected and demurred. Yet the counselor knew what to look for and pressed in. Finally the breakthrough came and with a stunning confession.

Martha: Do you have to tell my parents?

Counselor: I am forbidden to tell them.

Martha: They're paying you, aren't they?

Counselor: It doesn't matter. I will not tell them or anybody else.

Martha: Ever?

Counselor: Never.

Martha: My roommate...

Counselor: What about her?

Martha: She...I mean we...

Counselor: You what? You can tell me anything, Martha. You will not shock me.

Martha: I'm not a lesbian. *Weeping, shaking her head, and gripping the arms of her chair.*

Counselor: I see. Is that what happened?

Martha: She was nice to me. I just wanted to be friends. The next thing I know...we were...Oh God. I can't stand to think about it.

Counselor: How many times?

Martha: Once! My God, I'm not a lesbian! Just once.

Counselor: You don't think your parents can forgive that?

Martha: Never.

Counselor: Maybe they could. They seem to love you very much.

Martha: That's the one thing they can't forgive.

Counselor: Is it? What makes you say that?

Martha: I know what they believe.

Counselor: They believe in a God of grace, don't they?

Silence. Her head down.

Counselor: Well, don't they?

Martha: *Softly, hardly above a whisper,* I guess.

Counselor: You guess? What about you? Do you think God forgives that? Let's look at 1 John 1:9.

Martha: I know what it says.

Counselor: But you don't believe it?

Martha: Not for that. My father is a minister, and in our denomination fallen ministers can be restored for any sin except...

Counselor: Homosexuality?

Martha: Yes. *A sob from deep within her.* Homosexuality.

Counselor: I don't know what your denomination believes about restoring ministers, but I know what 1 John 1:9 means. It says God will forgive us and cleanse us of all unrighteousness. All unrighteousness. All has to mean all.

Martha just shakes her head, weeping softly.

Counselor: Do you hear me, Martha?

Silence. Weeping. Nothing more.

There was no breakthrough. There was no shining, liberating moment. Weeks later the counselor wept with Martha's numb and confused parents at the funeral. He could not comfort them. He could not explain to them why their beloved child had killed herself. He could not bring himself to tell them that what she perceived about their attitude toward that one sin was what helped put the rope around her neck. Could they have ever considered the possibility that the way they talked about homosexuality in their home became what she believed about getting or not getting forgiveness and healing from God?

Martha was a lonely girl who gave in to a single moment of what felt at the time like tenderness and intimacy. In the light of the morning afterward, she was left with nothing but an unspeakable horror that she had stepped over the line with God and her parents and that there was no going back. She couldn't live with the life of secrecy she knew lay ahead of her if she wanted to keep her parents' love. She couldn't live with a churchgoing life while knowing that the God of her parents' church despised her. That's all she was left with. That and the despair. Condemnation killed Martha.

THE THRONE OF IDOLATRY

"I know God has forgiven me, but I cannot forgive myself."

Every counselor has heard this. Condemnation is a powerful inner wound. Self-loathing, even self-destructive impulses, are rooted in condemnation. The horrible double hurt of sexual trauma rests squarely in condemnation. This was Martha's tragic story. *Someone did a filthy thing to me. Therefore, I am filthy. Therefore, I do that which is filthy. I am condemned for what I do, which is because of what I am, which is the result of what was done to me.* A horrific cycle.

That cycle is enforced by a surprising dominion: idolatry. This is the empowering throne that imprisons its wounded victims in condemnation. If my wound or my sin is bigger than God, or if my judgment is more righteous—that is idolatry. If I say that God forgives, but I cannot, then I claim to be a more righteous judge than God. This is the worst idolatry of all.

My triune idol—my pain, my wound, and my judgment—is the terrible "three in one." Addicted to pain, I deny God's healing power. Magnifying my wound out of all proportion, I make it bigger than any other wound ever suffered by anyone ever—bigger even than God Himself. By condemning myself, I dismiss God's grace as superficial, the bad decision of a weak old grandpa figure in heaven. My judgment, mine alone, determines that my failure is the unforgivable sin. If I judge better than God, then I must know more than He does, and I must therefore be better than He is. That is the idolatry of self.

Please remember this: condemnation is a toxic kind of idolatry that puts what I feel or believe ahead of what God says.

Our old friend Johnny labored manfully in this arena. He was already a believer when, out of his buried trauma, he acted in ways he believed to be sin. This inner dissonance condemned him. His inner "oughts" haunted him. *A believer* ought *not sin, and a believer* ought *not be forgiven when he does. God* ought *to cast him out.* This is what Johnny believed.

Scripture simply bounces off of such a belief system. This is particularly true of verses such as, "If we confess our sins, he is faithful and just and will forgive us our sins and purify us from all unrighteousness" (1 John 1:9, NIV).

Johnny's counselor guided him to see God's promised forgiveness as greater than a believer's sin. Johnny's remorse made his failure appear bigger than any life, bigger than any other sin ever committed, worthy of domination, and too big for God to forgive. Recognizing that remorse is healthy to an extent, the counselor had to proceed carefully. The remorse had to be affirmed. Yet Johnny also had to be talked down from the ledge of a legalistic view that once a person becomes a believer, his willful sin is unforgivable. He had broken the law, he believed. No forgiveness was possible. Still, gradually, Johnny came to see that his magnified view of his own failure was a kind of idolatry. He began to realize that if forgiveness was not true for everyone and everything, then the Christian faith is a useless sham.

Having repented of the destructive actions that very nearly made him despair of his salvation, Johnny then had to repent of the idolatry of his own opinions that made God into a wrathful, graceless being. Johnny learned that while condemnation is toxic and can be lethal, it is treatable. He learned that the therapy for this kind of idolatry is worship.

The problem is that when a word such as *worship* is used, it takes on different meanings depending upon context. For some, high church liturgies come to mind. For others, Pentecostal-Charismatic singing and clapping is suggested. Nearly all Christians think of the Sunday morning experience. Yet this is not what is meant here by *worship*. Instead, the focus of worship in this therapeutic context is to turn the eyes of the broken off of themselves in a focused manner that moves first upward and then outward. This is especially important for those suffering from the toxin of condemnation.

THE THERAPY OF WORSHIP

Let me say it again: The key to breaking the self-idolatry of condemnation is the therapy of worship. Worship would hardly be considered a legitimate therapy by many conventional counselors, but it is nevertheless a teachable, practical approach to healing the inner wound of condemnation. Worship, in short, restores the perspective needed to break condemnation.

The emotionally damaged are often referred to as unbalanced. Perhaps no word is more apt. The purpose of inner healing is actually the restoration of balance. Healthy emotions can be felt without exaggeration and expressed without extravagance. Damaged emotions find bizarre expressions—destructive expressions that yield control to further damage.

By restoring perception, internal calm, and an other-centered worldview, a worshipping life becomes a more balanced life. It could be said that all mental illness is to one extent or another an imbalance of self-centeredness: loving one's self too much, too exclusively, or too little. This is, in short, an imbalanced obsession with one's own emotions. All these imbalanced life issues are touched by the therapy of worship. Worship restores an external perspective. It also trains me to look outward by first looking upward.

Worship is therapy, and like any therapy it requires discipline. An athlete with a sports injury will enter a rigorous program of rehabilitation without asking himself questions about things like sincerity. He does not worry whether his "heart is in it." He simply plunges into the routine, believing that the long-run outcome of the repetitions will be therapeutic. Sometimes the therapy of worship will seem stale and unrewarding in the short run. The counselor must urge the wounded heart on "religiously."

Just do the repetitions! Lift the weight! Read the Scripture. Sit-ups. One, two, three. Copy that verse. Say it again. One more time. One, two, three. Lift, work, memorize, jog, meditate. Say it aloud. Again and again and again!

Dark, imbalanced self-absorption can be attacked and pulled down with a therapy of hard work. This occurs when the therapy of worship is at work. Daily forcing one's thoughts upward and outward from under the dominion of self is hard emotional work. The fruit of that therapeutic work is balance for wounded emotions.

In Johnny's hard work in this area, he discovered three aspects of worship that transformed his life:

1. *Gratitude.* Johnny's success in the corporate world had opened the door for a creeping sense of entitlement. The near loss of his family and the embarrassment over this at his company brought a needed brokenness to his life. Out of Johnny's brokenness the therapy of worship brought a new level of gratitude and intimacy.

2. *Humility.* The trauma of his youth produced in Johnny a hard self-dependence and self-confidence that often expressed itself as cockiness or arrogance. This is a defense mechanism that is resistant to true humility. In Johnny's deep subconscious, humility and humiliation were too painfully associated. The therapy of worship ushered him past traumatizing humiliation and into healing humility.

3. *Other-centered living.* Trauma produced in Johnny a strong impulse toward self-protection. In other words, the factors hindering the development of true humility, namely self-dependence and self-confidence, combined with hypersensitive self-protectiveness, inhibited the cultivation

of "other-centered" living. This is very common among victims of abuse, especially sexual trauma.

It can express itself in opposite and equally destructive ways. The first, as in Johnny's case, is a kind of combative, "quick-to-fight-back" syndrome. It grows increasingly difficult to be sensitive, caring, and sacrificial with one's closest relationships when life is in a battle for self-protection.

The opposite expression is just as wounded. As Johnny hid and denied his pain, others wallow in it. Their pain becomes their universe, cutting them off from the pain and needs of those around them. Like the combative Johnny, still refighting that one lost battle of his childhood, they live in an ambivalence of loss. The result is the same. Wrapped in a shroud of their own pain, they lose other-centeredness. The loss of intimacy that causes simply serves to reinforce their sense of lonely, self-absorbed pain.

Worship is, by definition, other-centered, or, more precisely, Other-centered. Worship serves to focus life, energy, and relationship beyond the wounded inner child wailing constantly for either protection or sympathy. If the wounded can fasten first their energy and later their affection on a greater and more worthy Other, their self-absorbed cycle of disconnection can be broken.

Johnny: You know I go to church, don't you?

Counselor: What's that got to do with it?

Johnny: You said we were starting some kind of worship therapy.

Counselor: Yes, that's right.

Johnny: Well?

Counselor: Well, what?

Johnny: Well, doesn't going to church have something to do with...

Counselor: I doubt it. Maybe for some people, perhaps, but my suspicion is that you do not worship much in church.

Johnny: I don't jump up and down, if that's what you mean.

Counselor: That is not what I mean. In fact public worship as a whole is not what I mean. It may even be the opposite of what I mean.

Johnny: What do you mean?

Counselor: I mean a disciplined approach to staring into something bigger and better than you are.

Johnny: You mean I should stand at the bottom of Niagara Falls every day and take stock of its power?

Counselor: I know you're being facetious, but actually that wouldn't hurt you one bit. But what I mean is to worship God, of course. A daily discipline of getting your mind off yourself and onto Him. It will not be easy for you.

Johnny: Why not?

Counselor: Because you have thought of very little else except yourself for most of your life.

Johnny: I suppose you're right.

Counselor: I am right. That's what you're doing right now. You're only thinking of how it made you feel for me to say that.

Johnny: How does this worship therapy work?

Counselor: Take this; it's called a journal. Here is a list of daily scriptures. Every day read the scriptures, think about them, really meditate on them, and then pray. It's OK to ask God for things occasionally, but don't do it all the time. Focus most of your time on only two things.

Johnny: What two things?

Counselor: God and others.

Johnny: Pray about God?

Counselor: Pray about God to God. That's worship. Concentrate on how wonderful God is. Think about it. Talk to Him about it. Lots. Then pray for others.

Johnny: God and others?

Counselor: That is the therapy.

Johnny: That's it?

Counselor: That's it.

Johnny: I can do that.

Counselor: I hope so. You never have.

Johnny: You're a real hardnose, you know that?

Counselor: I've been told.

MILTON'S STORY

Milton came to counseling after one too many family explosions. Thanksgiving at his in-laws' home had become a volcanic eruption when Milton lost his temper. Again. His in-laws hurting, his children embarrassed, and his wife threatening separation or divorce, Milton finally agreed to counseling.

Milton: I'm sick of this always being blamed on me.

Counselor: Is it always blamed on you?

Milton: Always.

Counselor: Why does that happen? Why is it always blamed on you?

Milton: Because I refuse to play the game. I won't just sit there and act like a doormat. I speak my mind.

Counselor: And you feel as if you have a right to speak your mind any way you want?

Milton: Everybody does. If they don't want to, that's their problem.

Counselor: Maybe they want to.

Milton: What?

Counselor: Just that. Maybe they want to explode too, and they don't.

Milton: Maybe they should.

Counselor: Maybe. But maybe if they did, the whole family would disintegrate. Maybe they think of it as self-control.

Milton: Again, that's their problem.

Counselor: You know, everybody is everybody's problem. There are no lines on a desert island. You are not just your problem. What about your kids? Your nieces or nephews? Your wife? Nothing in your family is just one person's problem.

Milton: Well, fine. Then it isn't all on me, is it?

Counselor: Probably not. But the only part you can fix is what is on you.

Milton: What about my father-in-law? What part can he fix?

Counselor: He can only fix his part, but he isn't here.

Milton: Well, we agree on that.

Counselor: But you are here.

Milton: Yes, I am. My wife doesn't seem to appreciate the fact that I'm the one here, not her perfect father.

Counselor: Is he perfect?

Milton: In her eyes he is.

Counselor: But not in yours?

Milton: Hardly. He disrespected me in front of the whole family. How does that get fixed?

Milton's father-in-law was the owner of a tool and die company. Milton had married the boss' daughter and risen through the ranks to become the vice president of sales. When Milton's brother-in-law got out of the navy, he was made regional sales manager without any consultation with Milton. The father-in-law later apologized, but the damage was done. An irreconcilable rift set in between Milton and his father-in-law and even more so between Milton and his brother-in-law. Now Milton's volatile emotions were so raw that at the slightest touch he would explode. The whole family lived in fear of these "Milton eruptions."

Milton began going to counseling begrudgingly but after a few sessions started to show such promise the counselor took him directly to the therapy of grace. Milton's sense of justice had been outraged and would not be easily healed. Apologies could be made. They could even be accepted, but the hated brother-in-law was still there. Milton had to find deep forgiveness, true forgiveness, for both of the offenders. He also had to forgive God for allowing such an injustice. He had to forgive his father-in-law for the disrespect, and he had to forgive his brother-in-law for being the "idiot son of a rich father who did not deserve his job." That is a lot of forgiveness for anybody, but for Milton's inflated sense of justice it was a high hurdle indeed. At last Milton found enough grace to grant grace, and he was well on his way to healing.

He moved on to mercy with less struggle. Having granted forgiveness to God and his in-laws, Milton received it himself. His natural bent toward legalism slowly gave way to a more merciful attitude. He began to realize that just as he needed mercy, so did his "idiot" brother-in-law and his softhearted father-in-law.

Milton's next step toward healing was made through the therapy of worship. Milton considered himself a "tough guy." He was somewhat contemptuous of emotions of every kind. Mushy sentiments? Not Milton. Romantic gestures? He sneered. Sometimes even common civility seemed to Milton like silly sentimentalism if not out-and-out hypocrisy. This is the constant challenge of wounded legalists: keep it real, or keep it to yourself. Being nice is a leap into the unknown.

Milton entered the therapy of worship a bit reluctantly but found, to his surprise, that he took to it. The counselor assigned him a Scripture reading schedule, mainly from the psalms. He journaled according to the assignment by writing down "nice things" to say to God and was then assigned to say those nice things to God aloud and alone. Over and over. Every day. Soon Milton found a liberty in private worship he never expected. Milton's next assignment was to transfer this fluency into his horizontal relationships. He was to translate the nice things he had said to God and similar comments to his wife, children, in-laws, and even "the idiots." Milton balked at this at first because of his inner battle with legalism.

Milton: You mean I was practicing on God?

Counselor: That's one way to put it.

Milton: Well, that doesn't seem right to me.

Counselor: No? It does to me.

Milton: Practicing on God seems right to you?

Counselor: Exactly. Everything we learn in private with God we are supposed to put into practice with people. Here's the rule: vertical first, then horizontal.

Milton: That's the rule?

Counselor: That's the rule.

Milton: It doesn't seem right to me, but I'll try it.

Try it he did. The remarkable thing to Milton was that as he got better at "nice things," his in-laws got nicer, but the goal was never for them all to become the best of friends. The purpose of the therapy of worship was to bring balance and self-control to Milton's life. His wife said worship restored their marriage and her sanity.

Milton: I'm very grateful.

Counselor: Good. Gratitude is part of worship too.

Milton: You know, in some ways he's still an idiot.

Counselor: Worship doesn't rid the world of idiots. It heals the people who need to learn how to live constructively in a world full of idiots.

Milton: When you started talking about the therapy of worship, I thought you meant singing in church.

Counselor: Singing in church should be about worship, but worship is not always about singing in church. Worship is about looking outside yourself. You start by looking up. The discipline of His Word, of praising Him...that's where worship starts. Then you translate that into how you treat people.

Milton: Surely you don't mean worshipping people.

Counselor: No, of course not, but learning how to move from private worship of God to a worshipful life. Your wife told me that you have started making the bed.

Milton: Every day.

Counselor: That is an act of sacrificial love for her. A self-absorbed man cannot do that just because it blesses her. He is too unbalanced.

Milton: Unbalanced? Was I unbalanced?

Counselor: Imagine you are on a boat. You and all your anger and hurt and unforgiveness are on one end, and nothing is on the other end. The boat tips. That's unbalanced.

Milton: And worship does what, exactly?

Counselor: It puts the weight of God in the other end of the boat. Your eyes are on Him. You focus in on Him. You become less, and He more.

Milton: Well, doesn't that unbalance the boat the other way?

Counselor: He is now in the boat, around the boat, under the boat, and in you. He is balance.

Milton: And making the bed—how does that figure in?

Counselor: Don't you see it? When your boat, your life, is unbalanced, you cannot love, you cannot serve and give and live a worshipful life because all the junk that is tipping your boat is all your life is about. With your eyes on God, your boat starts to balance. You can now see your wife's needs.

Milton: I have lived an unbalanced life.

Counselor: That is a very balanced thing to say.

Milton: I guess making the bed is a step.

Counselor: It's a good step in making your wife feel cared for. You must make her feel adored.

Milton: Adored?

Counselor: Adoration is part of worship. Haven't you ever heard a boy tell a girl, "I worship the ground you walk on"? Haven't you ever heard that?

Milton: Am I supposed to say stuff like that to my wife?

Counselor: Every day.

Milton: Every day?

Counselor: Every single day. Lots of times a day.

Milton: It sounds blasphemous.

Counselor: Milton, I thought we were past all that legalism.

Both God and your wife will understand the rhetorical difference between "worshipping the ground she walks on" and truly worshipping God. What is truly blasphemous is being so absorbed with your hurt and unforgiveness that you basically worship your own pain. That is blasphemous.

Milton: She likes it when I make the bed.

Counselor: Yes, Milton, she does. She bragged on you to me.

Milton: She did. Now what?

Counselor: Now notes.

Milton: Notes?

Counselor: Love notes, Milton. And candy. And gifts. Little acts of sacrificial worship... Worship with a small *w*.

Milton: I can do all that.

Counselor: Sure you can. Making the bed is a daily sacrifice.

Milton: Like lighting a candle at church.

Counselor: Exactly! Now move from that to adoration. The more you adore her and God, the more balanced your boat will become.

Milton: I need more balance.

Counselor: So does your wife, Milton. She is starving for it.

Milton: Adoration for balance.

Counselor: Adoration for her, and balance in you.

SELF-IDOLATRY

The power of condemnation rests in the throne of idolatry, self-idolatry. If I condemn myself, and if I am a better, more righteous judge than God is, I am utterly condemned. The lie underneath condemnation, the lie that makes this toxin so fatal, is the lie that says, "I cannot be forgiven because my sin is greater than the grace of God." That is quintessential idolatry. To think that my sin, my anything, is greater than the grace of God is to make an idol of my own wounded emotions.

Often this is an effort at penance. Condemning myself without mercy becomes my way of punishing my own sins. That's all about *me*. There is no room for God and His healing grace in that toxic formula. It is a lie, and it is a hellish lie.

What, then, is the truth that is the antitoxin for that lie? At first it may seem odd that worship is that truth. But think about it: if I am the biggest thing in my own life, if all I can see is my sin, my righteous judgment on myself and my unwillingness to believe for my forgiveness, the toxin of condemnation is inescapable.

Only when *me* is replaced by *Him* can worship happen. Likewise when worship happens, true worship of God, there is little room left for me. The biblical ground and foundation of all healing from condemnation is Exodus 20:3: "You shall have no other gods before Me."

It is from that great commandment that the healing from condemnation derives its power. If God is God, and He is, then I must worship Him as God. I cannot worship Him as God and not trust His Word above my guilt.

If I doubt His Word, I am not worshipping Him as God. All effective biblical counseling for the toxin of condemnation rests on who God is. If He is God, I must worship Him as God. I must believe Him and not my own wounded emotions. I must believe His love for me is greater than my contempt for myself. If not, I believe I am God.

If what I have done is greater than who He is, my sin, like a toxic golden calf, has supplanted God, and I am become my own terrible god. When I believe His Word and worship Him as God, condemnation is defeated. The healing antitoxin for condemnation and the lie on which it rests is the truth that God is God and is to be worshipped as God.

Chapter 7

THE TOXIN OF FEAR

TOXIN	THRONE	THERAPY	GOAL
Fear	Pain	Love	Hope

FROM HIS EARLIEST days fear never left Casey, never gave him a moment's rest. He functioned, kept a job, did what had to be done. He shopped. He drove. He graduated from college. He had the appearance of a life. He even went to church. Yet his life was consumed by fear.

Casey called it "worry." He worried about his parents. He worried about the economy, the government, and the company he worked for. If it went bankrupt, as so many have, whatever would he do? It appeared solvent, sure. But what if it did go under? Casey's entire life was a patchwork of these worries. What-ifs tortured him. He paced the floor. Insomnia racked him. His appetite came and went. He wrote out contingency plans, then threw them away and wrote others. He agonized over minor decisions. The fact that hardly any of Casey's fears ever materialized made no difference to him. His fears were compulsive, life-limiting, and destabilizing.

He finally met with a counselor because of a sermon he heard at church. That positive gospel message somehow brought Casey a ray of hope. When the counselor met Casey, he found his determination to live free of worry touching. The man had a can-do attitude, buoyed by that sermon he had heard. Yet Casey's fears made him inwardly such a jumble of contradictory emotions that his words were barely understandable: "What do you think? I mean you can help me, right? I mean, what about you? People don't, I mean, not everybody, at least, you know, they don't worry about, you know, I don't know for sure, but what do you think? I mean it probably isn't, well, I mean it couldn't get any worse, could it?"

This kind of confused, rambling monologue gushed out of Casey in the first meeting. Contrary to his experience with many of his clients, the counselor had no trouble getting Casey to talk. Indeed, he could hardly get Casey to stop talking. He tried to gently steer Casey back toward his earliest childhood fears or worries. This was not as easy as it sounds because Casey saw his entire life as a fearful trek through a lethal jungle. Isolating the start of the journey meant hacking through dense undergrowth of fears that were real, to be sure, but were not the headwaters of the damage.

At last the story began to emerge. When Casey was six, his father had deserted the family, which at that time was only Casey and his mother. This left his mother in dire financial straits, a topic she never ceased mentioning to her young son. She described in great detail all the possible consequences of this desertion and the resulting financial crisis. She even worried aloud that the state might come and take Casey away to an orphanage. It was a vision that festered in Casey's young mind and terrified him for years.

Casey recounted how he would lie awake at night, rolling these fears around in his head like a marble until he was exhausted. At school each day he battled to concentrate because of the dark scenarios playing out in his imagination. Later in life he called this "doing a worst-case scenario." He proclaimed that by processing his fears in this way, he could face the worst possible outcome. This may have seemed like a good coping mechanism at the time, but it proved to be quite destructive. He did not come up with practical strategies to handle these potential disasters. Nor did he emotionally process the possibility that the worst-case scenario might actually happen. He just lived in fear of it.

THE THRONE OF PAIN

Let me tell you the hard truth of fear, just as I have with the other toxins we've confronted. *Fear is seated in pain.* No one can fear the pain he is in. Present pain may be terrible to bear, but there is no fear in it except as the pain speaks of worse pain to come. Future pain, dreaded pain, finds its horror in either memory or imagination or both. This is just like when a child has an emotional meltdown in a doctor's office at the mere sight of a hypodermic needle. Why does this happen? It is because of an imagined level of pain to come informed by memories of pain in the past. Fear, a real and painful feeling, like an electric shock, connects to a fantasized future and runs like an electrical current through the conductor of the present. This is fear.

The problem, of course, is that the past can be as dark and murky as the imagined future. A memory can become so encrusted with pain that the precise order of events, the facts, can become confused and disordered. Pain is what reaches into the future and fuels fear, not facts. Until the pain—the memory of the pain, or, more precisely, the way that pain is— is remembered, the wounded, frightened child within cannot be healed.

The strange thing about pain is that we cannot remember how it actually felt when it was happening. We can remember that it hurt. The worse it hurt, the greater the pain and the more terrifying the fear that it would be repeated. Yet the actual sensation of the pain is not stored in our minds.

Pain is not alone in this. We cannot actually remember the smell of a flower—not exactly. We know that it smelled good. We recognize it when we smell it again. Yet if we could see our memories, the actual smell itself would not be there. Does that seem wrong? Try it. You have smelled roses; I know you have. Remember that smell. I know you remember it was a good smell. But the smell, that wonderful rose aroma, is not there, is it?

If someone lifts a bouquet of roses toward your face, you know it will smell good. You wait. Ah! There it is. You recognize it immediately, so you say you remembered it, but it is not "remembered" in the same way you can remember the words of a poem. Imagine if you said, "I know there are words. I know I liked them. I know I would be moved to read them again as I once was, but I cannot remember them."

Have you ever bumped your head? I mean, really hard. I

have. I did not care for it, and it is not a practice that I can imagine would ever be habit forming. Yet now, today, I cannot summon into my conscious mind the sensation of that pain—not the exact feeling of the pain. I do remember I wasn't fond of it. I also learned from it. When I stand up on airplanes, I try to remember that the luggage bin overhead is the implacable enemy of my poor head.

It's something like that with emotional pain as well. Just as the sight of an approaching bouquet of roses might put a spontaneous smile on your face, imagine if there were a thought—the sight of a certain face or a name—that shot paralyzing fear through you like a lightning bolt. Imagine to what ends you might go to avoid it. What is the source of the fear? It is pain. Our most dreadful fears are anchored in pain, yet it is not the pain itself that is so awful. It is the fear of the pain being repeated. You cannot remember the pain itself, not exactly, but this, whatever "this" is, reminds you of its unendurable agony, and at the very thought of it you are paralyzed. That is the toxin of fear, which rests on the throne of pain.

Here is the most difficult part about the connection between pain and fear: the fear does not always flow out of a traumatic experience of pain. In fact it may not even be connected to any experience, save that which exists in an overly fertile or unbalanced imagination. Childhood fears such as monsters in the closet fall into this category. Mostly such fears are common and entirely normal. Even so, they are rooted in pain, such as the imagined horror of being attacked or devoured by the beast under the bed. Indeed, the fact that such a nightmare has no real ground in personal experience is part of its terror. If a child does not even know what might happen, what it might feel like, what unspeakable agony such a monster attack *might* be like, then the fear of the unknown makes the fear greater.

To help her deal with it, the closet door must be opened. *See. No monster. No painful and horrendous experience is lurking in dark recesses.* Turning on the light dispels, at least temporarily, the awful possibility.

Imagined Pain

Some people who are in the grip of absolutely debilitating fear are not in that condition because of pain in the past but because of monsters in the closet. Their fears come from their own ability to imagine pain they have never endured, or, even worse, to imagine pain so unendurable that they cannot imagine it.

I spent a year counseling an older woman whose life was being severely limited by agoraphobia, the fear of being outside or in a crowd. She had never been assaulted, attacked, or abused. Her own son thought her fear was imaginary. Nothing could have been further from the truth. Her fear was the most real thing in her life. The base of her fear was what was not real. The great advantage I had in those sessions was her basic Christianity.

Over the course of that year, we worked very hard to let her faith override her imagination. All the horrors in her mind, such as social embarrassment and even violence, kept her locked in the house. That "spirit of fear" that was in her, a spirit of fear flowing out of pain (imagined though it was), had to be replaced with a new and sound mind of power and love. Her mind, her soul, would eventually have to be restored by love, but faith flowing out of the reality of God's omnipresence had to be the first step. We spent session after session just discussing the presence of God. In other words, if God is in the house and we are safe there, are we likewise safe in the yard because God is also there? In order to reinforce this, we began and ended every session with the Lord's Prayer and Psalm 23, reminding ourselves of God's presence and His protection.

Our next step was more harrowing for her. We actually considered the painful things that might happen to her outside. I actually pressed her into imagining pain. We went so far as to list terrible things such as car wrecks and assaults that could happen out in the world. Then we considered painful things that could happen in her house.

At one point she said, "Are you trying to make me *more* afraid?"

"Is that possible?" I asked her.

"I see your point," she said, and it was the first time I heard her laugh.

She had to see the disturbing reality that her house was hardly safer than the grocery store. There is always the possibility of pain. Everywhere. Anywhere. From there it was a short drive to the presence of God. We invited Jesus into all possible pain.

One day she said to me, "If pain is to be avoided at all costs, what about the cross?"

I immediately told her, "From this moment on, your healing will be at a whole new level."

And it was.

The first time her grown son found her outside watering the lawn, he was amazed. He told me later that even though he was delighted, he found the nonchalance and smug conde-scension of her rhetorical question more than a bit irritating. "Why shouldn't I be out here? Is God only with me in the house?" Eventually she was able to go to a shopping mall with her daughter. It was not total release, but it was a huge step.

The concept of faith was not the healing therapy she needed, but it was the beginning of that therapy. Her faith in the presence of God was the doorway. What she had to see, had to really embrace, was the love of that omnipresent God. The Bible says it this way: "Perfect love casts out fear" (1 John 4:18). God is there, in the yard, at the mall. That came first. Then came the great healing truth. He is not only *there*, He is there in perfect love. It is not the reality of God alone, nor just faith in His presence that heals our fears. It is rather that He who is present with us also loves us. When we finally invite Him to be present in our pain, real or imagined, He heals (casts out) our fears.

We spent some time inviting God to be in her house, room by room. In each room we praised Him for His love. Then we imagined His loving presence in the yard and in the mall and on the sidewalk. We invited Him into any place that she could likewise imagine being painful. We did not concentrate on the absence of pain but on the presence of God.

If imagined pain can limit a life in such an awful way, real pain, emotional or physical, can be devastating. Fear of pain, especially traumatic pain, can become a mental stronghold so dominant that it can be triggered by a sight, a word, a movie, or even a thought. What the mind wants more than anything in the world is to avoid the repetition of that pain. The fact that, just as we have said, the actual pain cannot be remembered is not the good part. That is the bad part.

Because I cannot remember the pain, I "imagine it backward," as it were, imposing on my memory the pain I imagine and, thereby, probably making it worse.

Now avoidance becomes the dominating reality of my life. I will run, withdraw, or fight. I will do anything to keep that pain at arm's length. Something may energize some small, even subconscious trigger in my mind, and the memory of that pain resurfaces like an electric shock. Now I'm off to the races. Fear like the hound of hell at my heels, I will do whatever it takes to keep that pain away. Rather than keeping the fear away, this actually increases my anxiety. Pain drives the fear. Fear drives the avoidance, and avoidance only makes it all worse.

One deeply depressed pastor told me of his painful childhood with an alcoholic father who horribly manipulated the entire family in gut-wrenching all-night "discussions," which left everyone emotionally drained. The father was not physically abusive, as are so many drunks, but his emotional abuse left deep and lasting scars.

The pastor's father would come home drunk at two in the morning and awaken the whole family, summoning them to the dining room table for a night of emotional pain. "You don't love me," he would yell at them. "None of you do. I may as well leave. I may as well kill myself. None of you love me. Not one of you!"

The poor little children, this pastor included, would try pitiably, with broken hearts and rivers of tears, to convince him otherwise: "We do love you. We really do. Please don't leave. Please don't kill yourself. Please believe us."

These horrible sessions would go on for hours. In the morning the father would go to bed to sleep it off, while his poor family would try to go on with life. The children, now beyond exhausted, had to go to school. The pastor told me this nightmare emotional merry-go-round was utterly fatiguing. It was also the number one issue in his counseling. He did not struggle, as so many do, with believing God loved him. He deeply believed that. His wearying and fruitless fight was to convince God of his love. He subconsciously saw God as a drunken neurotic father crying, "You don't love Me." No matter how he told God, "I love You," it seemed to him that God would say, "No, you don't."

The source of his pain was his father's neurotic and totally unreasonable denials of his family's love. When we met, he was trying to avoid the repetition of exactly that pain. He was hoping his deep spirituality, devotion, ministry, worship, and every other means the church afforded would finally convince God of his love. The therapy, the only therapy that could ever help him, was love. He had to see that true love can also be loved, can accept love. If God is perfect love, and He is, He loves us perfectly. Also, because He is perfect love, He accepts and fully receives our imperfect love. We need not convince God of our love. Indeed, we cannot. Pain is the source of all fear, and the therapy, the only therapy that casts out fear, is love.

The Therapy of Love

Consider the direct connection between past pain and feared future pain. In other words, the dread, the fear of possible pain in the future, arises straight out of painful memories of the past. The hope of healing fear actually lies, therefore, in healing the painful memory. The medicine must be the right medicine. Just as important, the right medicine must be applied to the right place. As stated, the healing of fear is in the healing of painful memories. There is only one medicinal flow strong enough for the healing of memories: love. Love heals painful memories where fear is anchored. Not just any love. Not just any kind of love. Only perfect love, or more to the point, perfect Love. Perfect Love heals memories; therefore, perfect Love casts out, or heals, fear.

The counselor began working with Casey to help him grasp that "perfect love casts out fear." This was the first stage of the therapy of love, the acceptance that the medicine for fear is love. The second step was identifying the source of Casey's fear: pain. In his work with the counselor Casey began to dredge up those painful days of his childhood. He remembered the pain-wracked little boy marinating in his mother's fear and loneliness. There, right there, is where the therapy of love has to be applied.

Casey: Now, it's all fine and good for us to say that love has to be applied to the point of the pain. But that's all just words. It's not like we can squeeze love out of a tube onto a cut.

Counselor: You know, Casey, that's not a bad metaphor.

Casey: What in the world are you talking about?

Counselor: Well, let's suppose there was such a thing, a tube of perfect love. Suppose there was. And that tube could be popped open and squeezed out onto our places of pain. What would happen is the reversal of what you have struggled with your whole life, at least since your father left. Your pain, your deepest memory of pain, is that moment of desertion and what you saw that it did to your mother. What you fear, what we all fear, is the repetition of that pain. It is there at the point of that pain where the love must be applied.

Casey: But how? What are you talking about? Can you "apply love" to a memory? You can't do that. Can you?

Counselor: Yes, Casey, you can. That is exactly what the cross is all about. That is where the vessel, the "tube," if you will, of perfect love was broken and poured out. The therapy of love is to get the cross into our most painful memory.

This is where they began. Through methods such as visualization, the counselor helped Casey see the cross in that horrible moment when his mother announced that they were on their own. In session after session Casey and his counselor prayerfully revisited those hysterical moments when the mother's fears rained down on a frightened child. They prayerfully reentered the heartbreaking scenes, each time armed with scripture.

"Father of the fatherless" and husband of the husbandless (Ps. 68:5).

"Lo, I am with you always, even to the end" (Matt. 28:20).

"I have loved you with an everlasting love" (Jer. 31:3).

They imaged these verses as holy ointment being poured on that frightened child, like oil upon his little wounded heart. Casey became the man healing the boy. He reached back to that child, pouring love on him, speaking to him as he was guided by the counselor.

Counselor: Come on, tell him about the love of God.

Casey: How? What are you talking about?

Counselor: Tell the boy within you; reach back through the years and tell him.

Casey: I'm not good at this kind of stuff.

Counselor: How do you know? Try, Casey. Let your sanctified imagination work. See that child.

Casey: You mean me.

Counselor: Yes, but not you now, you then.

Casey: Do you mean first talk to myself?

Counselor: No, I don't mean that. I mean talk to a boy, a frightened little boy who needs comfort.

A long silence. Painfully long. The counselor waits. This cannot be rushed. Tears. A deep sigh. Then he starts.

Casey: Don't be afraid.

Counselor: That's good, Casey. Real good. Go on.

Casey: It's going to be all right. Don't be afraid.

Counselor: Why not, Casey? Tell him.

Casey: Because...because...you are loved.

A sob. A deep sob.

Counselor: *Whispering,* Yes, Casey. Tell him again.

Casey: You are loved. You are loved. You are loved.

Counselor: Who loves the boy?

Casey: Who?

Counselor: Yes, who?

Casey looks up. The question is a surprise to him. An awakening.

Casey: God is who. God loves you, so there's nothing to be afraid of. She's not going to...

Now the counselor is surprised. Casey's eyes are closed. He shakes his head slowly from side to side. His voice is soft and warm. He almost coos to the boy within. The man comforts the wounded child within.

Casey: She's not going to. Don't be afraid. She's not going to.

Counselor: *Whispering,* Who, Casey? Who's not going to?

Casey: Mother.

Counselor: What is she not going to do?

Casey: Leave. Mother is not going to leave too. God loves you. Don't be afraid.

He looks up. A soft smile.

Casey: I'm not. I'm not afraid.

Counselor: Perfect love.

Casey: Yes, perfect love casts out all fear.

THE FRUIT OF LOVE

Fear attaches itself to pain like a barnacle to the bottom of a boat. Perfect love cuts it away, casts it out. In the place where that fear once was, in that terrible, damaged memory of pain, a new thing can grow. God's love is perfect. Its effect is to cast out, or heal, fear attached to pain. Its fruit is hope. As long as the pain of that memory remains unhealed within my damaged emotions, hope cannot flourish. Fear crowds it out, chokes it as a weed chokes flowers. Fear looks backward, fixated on the past and seated in pain. Hope looks forward and rests in perfect love. If I am unloved, unhealed, staring backward to the solitary story of my own pain, I live under the terrible bondage of fear, fear that the past will also be the future. Fear that the same pain will come again. Fear that I will never be free. Never be healed. Never be a whole person.

When perfect Love comes into my most painful memory, fear is broken and cast out. Hope is the fruit that can now blossom where fear once reigned. Fear's dominion broken is like the end of a terrible winter, and hope is the springtime of my inner self.

Casey: I'm sleeping better.

Counselor: That's great, Casey.

Casey: And I'm thinking about taking a cruise.

Counselor: Really?

Casey: You think I shouldn't?

Counselor: Well...

Casey: Well, what? Is a cruise a bad idea?

Counselor: All that water. Ships sink.

Casey: They do?

Counselor: Sure. Ever heard of the *Titanic*?

Casey: Oh, I get it. I didn't think counselors were supposed to mock people.

Counselor: Sometimes they are supposed to. Light, friendly mockery. I took a course in mockery when I was in graduate school.

Casey: So you think a cruise is OK?

Counselor: I think you thinking it's OK is wonderful.

Casey: Why?

Counselor: A cruise is something to look forward to, not worry about. Don't you see?

Casey: Yes, I do. I hope it will be fun.

Counselor: That's miraculous, Casey!

Casey: Fun?

Counselor: No, hope. Listen to yourself. You said, "I hope it will be fun. I hope..." Those are the two most miraculous words you've said since your father left.

Casey: I hope?

Counselor: Yes, Casey.

Casey: Does one hope, or does one have hope? Which is it?

Counselor: I think that is a wonderful thing for you to chew on.

Casey: Is that my next assignment?

Counselor: No. The cruise is. When we meet again, I want you to bring me a list of things you hope will happen on the cruise.

Casey: I might meet a nice woman.

Counselor: Look out.

Casey: What? Is that a bad thing to say?

Counselor: A woman? Lots to worry about there. Lots.

Casey: I bet you made an A in that mockery course.

Counselor: Hope, Casey. Say it a thousand times a day.

Casey: I hope.

Counselor: Yes.

Casey: I hope. I really do.

Hope and the Psychology of Promise

Despite all the damage we sustain in our emotional journeys, we still hope for wholeness. When that hope hemorrhages and finally dies, the emotionally damaged give in at last to the damage and the hurt done to them. Fear wins its final victory. When hope dies, despair rushes in to close the deal for damage.

The promises of Scripture are a powerful tool to fuel hope. The psychology of promises finds its greatest strength, of course, in receiving faith. Believers who accept the promises as exactly that, the promises of God, accept the hope they bring.

So powerful are these scriptural promises that even those who have no faith in God often receive hope from Scripture nonetheless. These scriptures can be "prescribed" in a positive way, as the counselor did with Casey: "Read these. It doesn't matter if you believe in the Christian God. Just take the words at face value. A lot of people who don't believe in God find these words encouraging. It can't hurt you."

Wounded emotions on the verge of despair are not nearly as resistant to words of promise as many think. Counselors who offer promise gently and with genuine concern may well find a surprising receptivity. Scripture is a rich mine of hope and positive reinforcement. Hope for the future is good psychology. Period.

Counselor: We are starting into a new step of therapy.

Casey: *Apprehensively,* We are?

Counselor: Don't be scared. It's a good step. This step was not possible before.

Casey: Why not?

Counselor: Because you weren't ready.

Casey: I wasn't?

Counselor: No.

Casey: But now I am?

Counselor: Yes. Isn't that great?

Casey: I suppose.

Counselor: Trust me, it is great.

Casey: What is this new step?

Counselor: We have to start reprogramming your onboard computer. Your mind is a hugely complicated computer, and like all computers it can only "think" with the information it is given.

Casey: Garbage in, garbage out.

Counselor: Exactly. So we have to start giving your emotions some new programs. Do you have a Bible?

Casey: No. I told you, I'm not a Christian, and I don't want you to save me. I told you that.

Counselor: I understand. I can't save you in the first place.

In the second place, I have found that wisdom can come to us from some strange sources. Have you ever found that to be true?

Casey: Yes, actually I have.

Counselor: You don't have to believe the Bible the way some people do in order to find wisdom in its pages. Does that sound reasonable to you?

Casey: OK. I can agree with that. As long as you're not trying to make me a Christian.

Counselor: Look, here is a list of what we might call "words of wisdom." Your emotions have been filled with damaging words of dark discouragement. Read these every day, and they will begin to awaken some hope. Look at the first one. Read it aloud.

Casey: "It is good that we should hope." Is that in the Bible?

Counselor: You see the reference there. "It is good that one should hope and wait quietly for the salvation of the LORD." That's Lamentations 3:26.

Casey: Lamentations. Well, that actually sounds like my whole life.

Counselor: Well, that little word of wisdom says even in a lamentable life, it is good to hope. You don't have to believe in God to see the positive good of putting that down into your emotions.

Casey: I suppose. My mother always told me that hopes were bad because they never come true.

Counselor: Maybe she had hopes and wishes mixed up. You might need a new program in that computer of yours.

Casey: Maybe I do.

Counselor: You do.

Casey: You're not trying to save me?

Counselor: That's beyond my scope. That's somebody else's work.

THE MONSTER IN THE BASEMENT: THEN AND NOW

Perhaps the most difficult task the counselor faces with many of the wounded is separating past, present, and future. St. Paul speaks of it in Philippians 3. He says that his approach to life is leaving the past behind and pressing forward purposefully. Paul was right, of course, but it is often easier said than done. A "past" that overshadows the present casts a dark cloud over the future.

One of the most strenuous of all disciplines for our wounded emotions is the assignment of the past to the past. "That was then; this is now" sounds like a mere platitude, but achieving this perspective in a healthy fashion is strenuous emotional work. One of the things that makes it so taxing is the constant nature of the discipline. "Then" keeps bubbling to the surface, oozing into "now" like the toxic waste it is. "Then" sours or even poisons "now" and threatens the future, and it never quits. A thought, a smell, or a scene in a movie, and "then" raises its ugly head with a vengeance.

Compartmentalization is not the answer. We cannot simply wall off whole parts of our lives. Denial may actually work for a season. The mind is an amazing organ, able to create a new history, revise the facts, and turn its back on "then" pretty stubbornly. But it won't work forever. "Then" is even more stubborn than our denial, more stubborn in fact than all our coping techniques. "Then" is the poison in the system, an opportunistic disease awaiting its moment. When stress, anxiety, a breakdown of relationships, failure, or a host of other weakening abilities occur, "then" is ready to attack. And attack it will.

Johnny, whom we have met often in these pages, walled off his traumatic experience. He made denial work for him for decades. Eventually, however, in a season of emotional stress and spiritual fatigue, the horrific scene pressed upward against the floor of his life like a monster in the basement. Johnny's last desperate attempts at denial and compartmentalization finally failed, and Johnny found himself deeply depressed, coldly isolated from Jenny, and depleted. The monster was loose, and it threatened to destroy Johnny's entire world.

"Then" must be embraced. The trapdoor must be opened, and the monster acknowledged before the monster forces its way out. It is painful to voluntarily see the monster in the basement, but it is far better than having it fight its way out. Once "then" is seen, called by its name and embraced as a real part of the story, the monster is defanged. The problem with monsters is that they can grow new fangs.

How do we continue to deal with "then" without lapsing back into the denial that leads to disintegration? By assigning "then" its proper place in the wholeness of my life. "Then" need not disappear, will not disappear. I must embrace it. It, whatever it is, happened. It cannot be denied. It cannot be kept imprisoned in the basement. "Then" is part of my life, but it need not have power over my "now." The toxic power of "then" is neutralized when "then" is put in its proper place.

When St. Paul said he "forgets" those things that are past, he cannot mean actually blocking them from memory because he very well remembers his past, including his complicity in the murder of Stephen. Indeed, he references this episode several times in his testimony. It would be utterly unlike Paul to indulge himself in denial, let alone recommend that practice to others.

No, he means something quite different. He uses "forget" to mean relegate. I relegate those things that are behind me to the past, as in "that was then." We must sort through the comprehensive whole of our lives, and while not denying our past, we make the decision, consciously, as to which suitcases we carry into the future. Those things happened. They happened to me, "then." I accept them as part of my story, but I will not live under the dominion of those memories. They are behind me. They are there, accepted—named, integrated into my life—but relegated to the past in terms of their power to touch my present or cloud my future.

This takes a tremendous level of psychological and spiritual discipline. It is also a life process. Indeed, look at St. Paul's language as he describes his discipline in his own life.

"But one thing I *do*..." (Phil. 3:13). Not did. Do, as in keep on doing.

"Forgetting" (v. 13). I go on "forgetting." I refuse on a daily basis to allow those memories to haunt. I do not deny they happened. I deny their poison access to my "now."

"I press toward the goal" (v. 14). No past tense here. I move on. I keep moving. Intentionally. My life is not some pathetic victim's trail of tears. I am pressing forward, seeking a goal, a vision, the purpose of my future. I cannot, I will not, lug wounded emotions with me into that future.

GOD'S ULTIMATE PROMISE

It is not God's will that I drag the burden of my past around all my days. There is no progress in that. Nor does God expect me to just "buck up and be a big boy."

"Not by might nor by power, but by My Spirit," we are told (Zech. 4:6).

Our God is a God of healing grace. He knows all the trauma, every hurt and each little wound that haunts the back alley of our tortured emotions. He will not abandon us to our own devices. Quite frankly our own devices are doomed to failure. Our wounded emotions create coping mechanisms such as denial, suppression, and compartmentalization to keep the monster in the basement, but any long-range healing comes with God's help.

He who is full of grace and power can heal our wounded emotions and make us whole people. He "charms our fears" and "bids our sorrows cease," says the great hymn "O for a Thousand Tongues to Sing."[1] There is no heart so full of hurt or hate that God cannot make it whole. Johnny, Jenny, Edith, and countless others who have the Wonderful Counselor discovered what it means that He makes the wounded whole. You can too.

The throne, the dominion upon which fear rests, is pain. The enemy of our souls dangles pain before our eyes like a lash. "See that?" he howls. "That is what's coming to you! Again and again and again!" The pain that Satan scares us with in the darkest night, that unavoidable pain, is the throne on which your fears reside, and that fear is toxic indeed.

What, then, is the lie that gives the throne of pain its power? That I am helpless before the pain. Just that. Helplessness gives pain its power, which becomes the toxin of fear that flows in damaged emotions.

The truth that heals our fears is not the end of pain. There is pain in life, it is true. Pain-free living is a false hope. It is not the end of pain that sets me free. What sets me free is love that casts out fear. First John 4:18 is the basis of biblical counseling for fear. I have seen that passage, along with 2 Timothy 1:7, do wonders in the lives of those crippled with fear.

> There is no fear in love. But perfect love drives out fear, because fear has to do with punishment.
> —1 JOHN 4:18, NIV

> For the Spirit God gave us does not make us timid, but gives us power, love and self-discipline.
> —2 TIMOTHY 1:7, NIV

I have likewise seen Psalm 23, applied lovingly, patiently, and medicinally, bring incredible healing to people who were incredibly toxic with fear.

> The LORD is my shepherd, I lack nothing. He makes me lie down in green pastures, he leads me beside quiet waters, he refreshes my soul. He guides me along the right paths for his name's sake. Even though I walk through the darkest valley, I will fear no evil, for you are with me; your rod and your staff, they comfort me. You prepare a table before me in the presence of my enemies. You anoint my head with oil; my cup overflows. Surely your goodness and love will follow me all the days of my life, and I will dwell in the house of the LORD forever.
> —PSALM 23, NIV

Many live with the horrible belief that life is good and God is hard. Hopeless fear is the inevitable fruit of that sad doctrine. It must be uprooted and this planted in its place: life is hard, even painful, but God is good. That is truth that sets the fearful free.

A WORD TO PASTORS

IT WAS SOMETHING of a surprise when my secretary said that the pastor of a nearby Presbyterian church was in the outer office requesting to see me. I had not met him before, though I had been in town by that time for nearly a year. When I first arrived, a few pastors, very few in fact, had stopped by to welcome me, but that tiny trickle had dried up months before. I wondered if this pastor might be a latecomer to that ever so small "welcoming committee."

He was a slight man whom I took to be in his late forties or early fifties. He reminded me very much of Mr. Rogers on the children's TV show, and I barely smothered a chuckle when he said he had come to welcome me to the neighborhood.

Our visit was brief enough, by his choice, even including the time it took for us both to have coffee. He declined anything to eat—even a cookie—and drank his coffee without sugar. I admired his resolve and supposed that his discipline was why he was so very slim. After his opening welcome,

he seemed at a loss for words, which I put down to the pro-
verbial Presbyterian reserve. Still, he was a pleasant enough
chap. All in all the visit was somewhat confusing, even to
the point where my secretary asked, "What do you think that
was about?"

Two hours later that pastor went into the study at his own
church, closed the door, put a gun in his mouth, and killed
himself. His little congregation, hardly more than a handful,
really, was in shock. His poor widow was devastated. I struggled with guilt. Had I missed something? Was his visit a
last-minute cry for help? It seems likely, but for the life of
me I couldn't remember anything he said that gave me the
slightest reason to think he was at such a low point. Had I
offered coffee and cookies to a man who was desperate for
something far greater? If he wanted more from me, he gave
no hint of it, or, more precisely, I failed miserably to pick up
on it.

I have, as you might imagine, searched my memory of that
brief visit and asked myself a thousand times if there were
shadows of pain in his eyes, some quiver in his voice to which
I should have been more sensitive. Did his hand shake as it
took the coffee cup from my smiling secretary? If it did, I
missed it, and so did she. In his soft "No, thank you" to the
Lorna Doone cookies, should I have heard a plea for help?
Perhaps. But I will never know.

What I do know is this: There are ministers and lay
Christians whose lives have slipped into a place of such smothered despair that at any moment the last thread threatens to
snap and plunge them into the abyss.

While hard statistics for addiction and suicide among clergy
are uncertain at best, most denominational professionals

agree that the reality is bleak and things are probably getting worse. As the executive director of the National Institute of Christian Leadership, I teach and spend time with hundreds of pastors every year. Many, not a few, but many, of them are deeply disheartened. They pour their hearts out to me, expressing their sense of inadequacy and fear, especially of being rejected by their own congregations. Quite often they share dark struggles with loneliness and depression. They talk to me because they know I understand. They know I have been there myself, and I've never made any secret of it.

In a Q and A session at one church someone asked about a handsome young pastor in California who took an extended sabbatical, only to commit suicide almost immediately upon his return. I was surprised and disappointed when a layman said, "I don't see how a Christian minister could ever get to the point of doing that."

"I do," I responded. "I've been right there with my toes over the edge of the abyss. And if ever once, even for a moment, you experience true depression and all that causes it and all the poison that oozes out of it, you will understand exactly how he got there."

The church must get serious about inner healing. Denominations must get serious about providing counseling for pastors, not just *after* a breakdown or a scandal but before. And pastors must get serious about seeking counseling before they face a crisis.

Here is the all-important truth: many who sit in pews and stand in pulpits Sunday after Sunday and who are deeply committed believers are in need of inner healing. And not all the healing they need is to be found at the altar or in the confessional.

This is a word to clergy, not about clergy. Wise pastors will ally themselves with capable, Spirit-led professionals to whom they can refer church members whose needs go beyond the average pastor's abilities, training, and time restraints. Many pastors, whether consciously or subconsciously, view professional counselors as irrelevant or as competitors—even as adversaries. At some point in the course of ministry, and more likely at a thousand points, every pastor will encounter lives tied up in internal knots. Knowing that such an encounter is beyond the scope of my skill and training is one thing. Being prepared to refer those in need is even better.

Consider again the story with which this book began, the poor wretch lowered through the roof in Luke chapter 5. Four men carried their friend to that place, where they realized two things: they could not get him in to see Jesus by conventional means, and they were insufficient to do the task themselves. That hardly made them failures. It made them do what it took to get their friend in a place to get healed. Referring those in need and following up is where the pastor becomes just such a friend. At some point we may recognize we have gotten a broken person as far as we can, to the limit of our gifts and training and, pardon the phrase, job description.

The four men on the roof did not abandon their friend. Nor did they just drop him through a hole in the roof. They lowered him carefully, even tenderly, into a place where healing was more possible than it was on the roof or on the street. Here's the thing many miss: the rooftop and the street were necessary steps in the journey.

Pastor, if God uses you to shift some wayward sheep from their shattered existence on the street upward to the rooftop, how great a joy is that. Well done, thou good and faithful friend. You have been used wonderfully in the healing process. To realize there is another step, another place for even more healing, is not to admit failure. Nor is it to cast aspersions on the previous steps. Look again at the steps.

1. *The street to the rooftop.* That must have taken some heavy lifting. Doesn't it always?

2. *The rooftop to the room below.* Recognition that the roof was not the end of the process. More heavy lifting.

3. *The first words of Christ:* "Your sins are forgiven." That must have been a disappointing thing to hear up on that roof. They had not hauled him up there and then lowered him down for forgiveness but for physical healing. But it was a necessary step in their friend's healing, a step not to be skipped over.

Do you see? The street led to the roof, and the roof to the ropes, and the ropes to the presence of Christ in a new way. Forgiveness led to faith, and faith to a physical miracle. Each step was necessary, and friends who could do the heavy lifting were essential to the process. When you do what it takes, and it often takes a lot, to get those who need it into a new place of healing, you are like the friends on the rooftop—you've done your part. You are being a faithful friend willing to undertake the humble task of heavy lifting. Once the person who needs healing is in the presence of Jesus, that person experiences *His* power. *He* does the healing.

Sufficient theological work must also be done to make room for the kind of inner healing that goes beyond crises at the altar. Salvation must be preached, and the empowerment of the Spirit declared and received. None of this even hints at compromise on preaching and expecting souls to be saved. Not in the least. Lost sheep must be sought and found and discipled. That must never change. But we must also take care of the sheep who haven't strayed but who have stayed home with all their inner fears and wounds and scars intact, unhealed and oozing toxins into the bloodstream of the church. We must also take into account that the lost sheep being gathered into the fold so wonderfully do not emerge from a life of sin unscathed. Being saved is one thing, and thank God for it. Being healed inside from the toxic life they have escaped may also be needed.

At a large leadership conference, after my message on dealing with stress, I met the president of a unique and creative nonprofit ministry. He began by telling me the remarkable story of his conversion in prison. It was an exciting and inspiring story, and he told it with passion, but suddenly, halfway through, he began to weep. Realizing people were watching, I maneuvered him around until his back was to the others milling about the front of the auditorium. He leaned against me and whispered, "I'm losing it. I mean it. The stress is killing me. I won't be able to do this much longer. At least not like this."

He was as committed a believer as I've ever met. His faith was not the issue. He didn't need to get saved again. Likewise he understood himself to have been filled with the Spirit. We didn't need to go there again. But as the brief conversation unfolded, I sensed I should ask him if his father was proud of him. At this his tears turned to bitter laughter.

"You'd think he would be, wouldn't you? Well, he's not. He

thinks what I do is a joke, and he thinks I'll fail at it. I'll prove him wrong if it's the last thing I do."

He knew he was stressed to the breaking point. He told me that with tears in his eyes. What he apparently could not see was that a major source of his stress was that he was living under the lash of proving his father wrong. When I pointed out to him that I thought spending some time with a counselor would be a tremendous blessing to him, he shrugged it off. "I don't know," he said. "If anybody needs counseling, it's my father."

"Perhaps," I said. "But he's not here. You are, and I think it would help."

What was the cause of his reluctance? His theology was part of it. He was a "front of store" minister. He was so passionate about sales that he had little or no patience for the service department or the body shop, of which he himself was in serious need. He spent so much time leading bikers, gang-bangers, and prisoners to Christ that he gave little thought to inner healing, his own included.

At the point where a pastor, or any leader, for that matter, needs the "service department," it need not be broadcast. I'm not suggesting some dangerous, career-threatening announcement from the pulpit. What I am suggesting, no, *urging* with all love and tender compassion, even as I understand the risk, is that if you need help sorting things out, things that may have lain untouched or even buried for years, find a confidential Christian counselor, and get on with that "sorting" process. It will take some courage, but far better to let courage be the catalyst than crisis.

Some years ago my wife, Alison, and I taught at a marriage conference at a church in a very religious college town.

After one session a sad young couple asked to speak with us privately. It was quickly apparent they were both in desperate need of healing. Their young eyes were filled at first with pain and then with tears. They were having serious trouble sexually, much of which was tangled up in their strict and unyielding religiosity. They were both also very immature. He was selfish, while she was so bound up in legalistic religiosity that she could hardly even genuinely express her own hurt. They had gone past the early stages where troubled couples blame themselves and were already at the point of blaming each other. The one thing they both agreed on was that their marriage was a disaster in bed, at dinner, and in the car—in fact everywhere except at church.

Alison suggested they both needed extended counseling, way beyond what we could do in such a brief meeting. They acknowledged they did but said they lacked the money for it. "We can't afford all that," the wife said. "Travel expenses, hotel rooms, professional counseling. We are students. There's no money for that kind of stuff."

I pointed out that in a college town there were bound to be psychology professors who could help, or counseling departments at the larger churches in town. I even joked with them that there were more churches of their denomination in that town than there were Catholic priests in the Vatican. They failed to see the humor. In fact, they were horrified.

"Here? In this town?" she wailed. "Are you crazy? We can't go to counseling here. My father is one of those pastors you're joking about. My husband's father is on the faculty at the college. Are you kidding? If we went for one counseling session, it would be all over town in an hour."

"Would that be so bad?" I asked. "Would it be so horrible

for that to be known?" They stared at me like the naive fool they obviously thought I was, and I felt a wall had come down that basically ended the conversation. I tried to press ahead, but it did not seem to breach or even dent the wall when I pointed out the obvious: if their marriage ended in a painful breakup, the whole town would know that too. In fact they seemed to be less afraid of divorce than that it be known they were going for counseling.

They lacked, insofar as I could tell, the courage to be healed. Was their religious community to blame? Perhaps to some extent. Their upbringing? Maybe. The contemporary church must do the hard work, especially, but not exclusively, in the pulpit, to validate the healing ministry of counseling and to remove any stigma attached.

The bottom line, however, was themselves. At some point the poor twisted soul being hoisted up the stairs by his faithful friends must either yell, "Let me down!" or take the risk and let himself be lowered right into the presence of healing love.

My dear fellow leaders, may God grant you the grace for the heavy lifting so that others may be healed. May He also grant you courage, the courage to be healed.

EPILOGUE

RECENTLY A MAN whom I did not recognize came up to me after I spoke at a conference in Atlanta. When he reminded me of the last time I had seen him, I remembered it with a slight twinge of embarrassment and some concern for what he would say next. Our earlier encounter had been through a marriage counseling session at Mount Paran Church, where I did more counseling than anywhere else in my career.

"My wife and I came to you for counseling, and I didn't get what I expected."

I did not doubt that in the least. I did something in that session with him I'd never done before or since. The session had begun badly and finally just became useless. This was almost entirely because of him. His arrogance and selfishness were so blatant, so brazenly flaunted, that I was stunned. I tried, as I remember it, to steer him to a place where he could see his wife as a person, a real person apart from her marriage to him. He couldn't. At least he wouldn't. She had no meaning to him except as she met needs in his life.

He ranted. She wept. I finally gave up.

"I'm going to write you a prescription," I told him. "I do not want you to look at it until you're alone. You don't ever have to show it to your wife. It's your prescription, not hers. It's like all prescriptions: If you take it, you can be healed. If you don't, it can't help you."

I thought of all this when he reminded me of who he was.

"Do you remember what you wrote?" he asked.

"Yes, I do."

He extended the note. It was my handwriting. I couldn't have denied it if I'd wanted to. I recognized it immediately. There it was. He had kept it for all those many years. Decades, actually. Just two words: GROW UP!

I wasn't sure what I should say. Should I apologize—for the exclamation point, if for nothing else? Instead, I just stood there sheepishly. He spoke first.

"This note changed my life," he said. "When I opened it in the parking lot, it was a slap in the face. I started to go back up to your office. Something stopped me. Instead, I've looked at this note almost every day for all these years. We are still married, and we are happier than I ever thought we could be. What do you think of that?"

"I think you are a courageous man," I said.

He was. It took very little courage for me to write that. A bit of attitude, perhaps, but not much courage. I felt bad about it the minute he left my office. It took great courage for him to take that slap in the face like a man and keep on taking it year after year until it slapped some sense into him. That's courage to be healed.

It isn't always that easy. Selfishness is one thing. A deeply wounded soul is another. Still, it will most often be courage that makes the difference.

One of the stupidest things we say to each other in painful times is, "I know how you feel." I make no claim of knowing how you feel. I don't know what you're facing even as you read these words. I don't know what you've been through, the pain you've experienced, the outrages inflicted upon you, or the losses you've endured. I certainly don't know how all those things make you feel. I do know this: no matter what you've experienced, no matter the shame or fear or toxic bitterness that has flowed across your soul, perhaps for years, no matter what secret lurks under the floorboards of your life, God can heal wounded souls.

King David, in Psalm 23, testified, "He restores my soul" (v. 3).

David was a man who knew a bit about a soul in need of restoration. He experienced grief, fear, rejection, betrayal, sin, guilt, condemnation, and very public shame. Not just embarrassment but a very real, very hard-core and front-page public scandal.

When David said, "He restores my soul," he was talking about the restorative grace of almighty God that can heal souls tortured and twisted beyond recognition. I may not know how you feel, but King David probably did. God certainly does. He knows exactly what you've been through. He knows about your most egregious sins and the worst sins ever committed against you, and He knows the damage it's all done.

Think once more of that poor crippled man in his bed up there on that rooftop, watching his friends tie ropes to the corners. They were ready to do whatever it took to get their friend into the presence of Jesus. Jesus Himself was just below with all the healing power of heaven in His every word. The stage was set. The mechanism of healing was ready. The source was present. One variable would either stand in the way or make healing possible: courage or the lack thereof.

At some point those four men, having tied the ropes to his bed, looked at their friend and asked him, "Are you ready?"

And you? Are you ready? Are you ready to get on with it at last? Are you ready to dig up the nasty stuff under the floorboards? Are you ready to finally take out the trash? Are you ready to leave childish things behind and grow into a whole new and newly whole you? Are you ready?

The man in the bed looked down through the hole in the roof. It was a long way down. What if they dropped him? Would this heal him or kill him? Look at all those people and that teacher staring up at him. Would he be raised up from his bed of affliction or just be mocked and rejected one more time? His friends looked at him. "Ready?" they asked again.

"Ready," he said. "Lower away."

That is courage to be healed.

NOTES

CHAPTER 1

1.   William Wordsworth, "My Heart Leaps Up," Academy of American Poets, accessed May 13, 2019, https://www.poets.org /poetsorg/poem/my-heart-leaps.

2.   Ronald Francis Hingley, "Joseph Stalin," *Encyclopaedia Britannica*, accessed May 13, 2019, https://www.britannica.com /biography/Joseph-Stalin.

3.   Gina Dimuro, "Origins of Evil: The Rage-Filled Story of Alois Hitler," All That's Interesting, accessed May 13, 2019, https://allthatsinteresting.com/alois-hitler; Stephen A. Diamond, PhD, "How Mad Was Hitler?" Psychology Today, December 20, 2014, https://www.psychologytoday.com/us/blog/evil-deeds /201412/how-mad-was-hitler; Daphne Merkin, "If Only Hitler's Father Had Been Nicer," *New York Times*, January 27, 2002, https://www.nytimes.com/2002/01/27/books/if-only-hitler-s -father-had-been-nicer.html.

4.   Ralph Diehl, "Legion," Pastor Ralph Diehl, accessed May 13, 2019, http://www.ralphdiehl.com/tag/c-s-lewis/.

5.   Brooke Lea Foster, "Helping Soldiers Heal," *Parade*, October 4, 2009, https://parade.com/49266/parade/091004 -helping-soldiers-heal/.

6.   George T. Wiley, "New York Yankees vs. Philadelphia Athletics, 1927-1932," Society for American Baseball Research— Research Journal Archives, accessed May 14, 2019, http:// research.sabr.org/journals/yankees-vs-athletics-1927-1932.

7.   Adam Augustyn, "New York Yankees," *Encyclopaedia Britannica*, accessed May 14, 2019, https://www.britannica.com /topic/New-York-Yankees#ref1030798.

8. "1927 New York Yankees Statistics," Baseball Reference, accessed May 14, 2019, https://www.baseball-reference.com /teams/NYY/1927.shtml.

9. "1927 New York Yankees Hitting Stats," Baseball Almanac, accessed May 14, 2019, http://www.baseball-almanac .com/teamstats/hitting.php?y=1927&t=NYA.

10. "The Pinstripe Press: The 1927 Yankees," Baseball Almanac, accessed May 14, 2019, http://www.baseball-almanac .com/articles/aubrecht2.shtml.

11. For more information see "1927 New York Yankees 'Murderers Row,'" Fold3 by Ancestry, accessed May 14, 2019, https://www.fold3.com/page/629784704-1927-new-york-yankees -murderers-row.

CHAPTER 3

1. "The Lord's Prayer," *The Book of Common Prayer,* accessed May 21, 2019, https://www.bcponline.org/General /paternoster.html.

CHAPTER 7

1. Charles Wesley, "O for a Thousand Tongues to Sing," Hymnary.org, 1739, https://hymnary.org/text/o_for_a_thousand _tongues_to_sing_my.

All revenue & royalties from Dr. Rutland's books
go directly to support the ministry of

globalservants

Serving others through
God's love in action.

WHAT WE DO...

- *Preventing Human Trafficking*
- *Building Girls Homes & Churches*
- *Digging Wells & Creating Village Hygiene Stations*
- *Providing Education & SO MUCH More!*

CONNECT WITH US!

@GlobalServants
globalservants.org

LEADERSHIP TRAINING THAT WILL CHANGE YOUR LIFE FOREVER

Session 1	Session 2	Session 3	Session 4
Change Dynamics	**Strategic Growth**	**Transformational Management**	**Communication & Worship**
Organizational Definition & Balance	*Building, Directing & Leading for Quality*	*Strategic Leadership for Growth*	*Excellence in Expression*

ENROLL TODAY!

For more information, please visit:
theNICL.com